GAYLORD MG

The Dred
Scott Decision

FAMOUS

TRIALS

Other books in the Famous Trials series:

The Dred Scott Decision

by
Bonnie L. Lukes

FAMOUS
TRIALS

Lucent Books, P.O. Box 289011, San Diego, CA 92198-9011

Library of Congress Cataloging-in-Publication Data

Lukes, Bonnie L.
　　The Dred Scott decision / by Bonnie Lukes.
　　　　p. cm. — (Famous trials)
　　Includes bibliographical references and index.
　　Summary: Traces the history of the landmark Supreme Court decision that defined the right of slaves in the United States.
　　ISBN 1-56006-270-3 (alk. paper)
　　1. Scott, Dred, 1809–1858—Trials, litigation, etc.—Juvenile literature. 2. Sanford, John F.A., 1806-or 7–1857—Trials, litigation, etc.—Juvenile literature. 3. Slavery—Law and legislation—United States—Juvenile literature. 4. Slavery—States—Legal status of slaves in free states—Juvenile literature. [1. Scott, Dred, 1809-1858. 2. Slavery—Law and legislation.] I. Title. II. Series.
KF228.S27L85　1997
342.73'087—dc20
[347.30287]　　　　　　　　　　　　　　　　　　　　　96-34419
　　　　　　　　　　　　　　　　　　　　　　　　　　　　CIP

Copyright © 1997 by Lucent Books, Inc.
P.O. Box 289011
San Diego, CA 92198-9011
Printed in the U.S.A.

Table of Contents

Foreword

"The law is not an end in and of itself, nor does it provide ends. It is preeminently a means to serve what we think is right."

William J. Brennan Jr.

THE CONCEPT OF JUSTICE AND THE RULE OF LAW are hallmarks of Western civilization, manifested perhaps most visibly in widely famous and dramatic court trials. These trials include such important and memorable personages as the ancient Greek philosopher Socrates, who was accused and convicted of corrupting the minds of his society's youth in 399 B.C.; the French maiden and military leader Joan of Arc, accused and convicted of heresy against the church in 1431; and former football star O. J. Simpson, acquitted of double murder in 1995. These and other well-known and controversial trials constitute the most public, and therefore most familiar, demonstrations of a Western legal tradition that dates back through the ages. Although no one is certain when the first law code appeared or when the first formal court trials were held, Babylonian ruler Hammurabi introduced the first known law code in about 1760 B.C. It remains unclear how this code was administered, and no records of specific trials have survived. What is clear, however, is that humans have always sought to govern behavior and define actions in terms of law.

Almost all societies have made laws and prosecuted people for going against those laws, but the question of which behaviors to sanction and which to censure has always been controversial and remains in flux. Some, such as Roman orator and legislator Cicero, argue that laws are simply applications of universal standards. Cicero believed that humanity would agree on what constituted illegal behavior and that human laws were a mere extension of natural laws. "True law is right reason in agreement with nature," he wrote,

6

world-wide in scope, unchanging, everlasting. . . . We may not oppose or alter that law, we cannot abolish it, we cannot be freed from its obligations by any legislature. . . .This [natural] law does not differ for Rome and for Athens, for the present and for the future. . . . It is and will be valid for all nations and all times.

Cicero's rather optimistic view has been contradicted throughout history, however. For every law made to preserve harmony and set universal standards of behavior, another has been born of fear, prejudice, greed, desire for power, and a host of other motives. History is replete with individuals defying and fighting to change such laws—and even to topple governments that dictate such laws. Abolitionists fought against slavery, civil rights leaders fought for equal rights, millions throughout the world have fought for independence—these constitute a minimum of reasons for which people have sought to overturn laws that they believed to be wrong or unjust. In opposition to Cicero, then, many others, such as eighteenth-century English poet and philosopher William Godwin, believe humans must be constantly vigilant against bad laws. As Godwin said in 1793:

Laws we sometimes call the wisdom of our ancestors. But this is a strange imposition. It was as frequently the dictate of their passion, of timidity, jealousy, a monopolizing spirit, and a lust of power that knew no bounds. Are we not obliged perpetually to renew and remodel this misnamed wisdom of our ancestors? To correct it by a detection of their ignorance, and a censure of their intolerance?

Lucent Books' *Famous Trials* series showcases trials that exemplify both society's praiseworthy condemnation of universally unacceptable behavior, and its misguided persecution of individuals based on fear and ignorance, as well as trials that leave open the question of whether justice has been done. Each volume begins by setting the scene and providing a historical context to show how society's mores influence the trial process and the verdict. Each book goes on to present a detailed and lively account of the trial, including liberal use of primary source material such as direct testimony, lawyers' summations, and contemporary and modern commentary. In addition, sidebars throughout the text create a broader context by presenting illuminating details about important points of law, information on key personalities, and important distinctions related to civil, federal, and criminal procedures. Thus, all of the primary and secondary source material included in both the text and the sidebars demonstrates to readers the sources and methods historians use to derive information and conclusions about such events.

Lastly, each *Famous Trials* volume includes one or more of the following comprehensive tools that motivate readers to pursue further reading and research. A timeline allows readers to see the scope of the trial at a glance, annotated bibliographies provide both sources for further research and a thorough list of works consulted, a glossary helps students with unfamiliar words and concepts, and a comprehensive index permits quick scanning of the book as a whole.

The insight of Oliver Wendell Holmes Jr., distinguished Supreme Court justice, exemplifies the theme of the *Famous Trials* series. Taken from *The Common Law*, published in 1881, Holmes remarked: "The life of the law has not been logic, it has been experience." That "experience" consists mainly in how laws are applied in society and challenged in the courts, a process resulting in differing outcomes from one generation to the next. Thus, the *Famous Trials* series encourages readers to examine trials within a broader historical and social context.

Introduction

Slavery in the Courtroom

Washington, D. C., Friday 11:00 a.m., March 6, 1857. An overflow crowd of spectators and journalists watched as the nine black-robed members of the United States Supreme Court entered the courtroom. The man who had started it all was not present. Dred Scott waited in St. Louis to hear whether or not he was finally a free man. It had been eleven years since he began his quest for freedom in a Missouri state circuit court.

Chief Justice Roger Brooke Taney took more than two hours to read the majority opinion of the Court in *Dred Scott v. John F. A. Sandford*. By a vote of seven to two, the Court declared that Dred Scott and his family were still slaves. And the Court ruled that African slaves were the private property of their owner and that no Negro, free

Roger Brooke Taney was presiding chief justice during the Dred Scott decision.

9

or slave, could be a citizen of the United States or even a citizen of a state. Furthermore, that section of the Missouri Compromise of 1820 that prohibited slavery in the federal territories was proclaimed unconstitutional.

Many in the nation were stunned by the verdict, not so much because Dred Scott had lost his chance for freedom, but by the Court's stand on issues beyond Dred Scott. Slavery had long been a subject of bitter controversy that divided the nation. Now the Supreme Court justices appeared to have taken it upon themselves to resolve the problem. Instead of ruling on the single question of freedom for one man, they ruled on, and apparently sanctioned, slavery in America. Or did they? Controversy raged. Did the opinion of the Court actually reflect the opinion of a *majority* of the Court, or was it the opinion of the chief justice only?

In Springfield, Illinois, a rising frontier politician named Abraham Lincoln declared, "We think the Dred Scott decision is erroneous. We know the court that made it, has often over-ruled its own decisions, and we shall do what we can to have it to overrule this."

At the outset, the Dred Scott case had appeared to be a simple one: a slave suing for freedom on the grounds that his master had taken him into a free state. Although most southern states had strict laws against manumission—denying an owner the right to free his own slaves—slaves themselves could sue for freedom. Many had sued on the same grounds as Scott and won. Considering such precedents, Dred Scott had an excellent chance of winning when he went to court in 1846. However, by the time the Supreme Court ruled on his case eleven years later, slavery had become a divisive and volatile political issue.

Dred Scott went to court seeking freedom for himself and his family. He could not have imagined that his case would result in one of the Supreme Court's most debated and controversial decisions. Nor could he have guessed that it would help precipitate a civil war—a war that would lead to the Thirteenth Amendment to the Constitution and the abolition of slavery in the United States forever.

The story of Dred Scott, then, is about much more than the freedom of one slave and his family. It is a story of mistakes and injustice that still stains our nation's history. It stands as a reminder of how even America's highest court can be affected by the political and social problems of the day.

Chapter 1

A Slave Named Dred Scott

DRED SCOTT WAS BORN OF NEGRO SLAVE parents around the year 1800. Like most slaves Scott's parents were illiterate, so little is known about his early life. No one even recorded his date of birth. He was owned by Peter and Elizabeth Blow of Virginia, but it is not clear if they were his original owners. It is known, however, that when the Blow family settled in St. Louis, Missouri, in 1830, they brought Scott with them.

Then, in 1831, Dred Scott's circumstances changed. That year both Elizabeth and Peter Blow died. And sometime before December 1833, Scott was sold to a physician living in St. Louis. Because no bill of sale exists, it is uncertain whether Peter Blow himself sold Scott or his oldest daughter, Elizabeth, sold him out of her late father's estate. In any case, Scott became the property of Dr. John Emerson and began the travels that would lead him to the Supreme Court.

Dred Scott on the Road

In 1834 Dr. Emerson obtained a commission in the U. S. Army and was assigned to Fort Armstrong in Illinois. The Northwest Ordinance had made slavery illegal in the state of Illinois, but Emerson disregarded the ban and took Dred Scott along as his personal servant. Two years later, Emerson transferred to Fort Snelling in free Wisconsin territory (now Minnesota). Again he took Dred Scott with him even though the Missouri Compromise prohibited slavery there.

12

Fort Snelling on the upper Mississippi during the time Dred Scott met and married Harriet Robinson.

At Fort Snelling, Dred Scott met and married Harriet Robinson, a young black woman in her middle teens. She was the slave of a federal agent at a nearby Indian agency. After the marriage, Dr. Emerson acquired ownership of Harriet. Eventually, he would also own the two daughters produced from the Scotts' marriage.

Late in 1837 the army reassigned Emerson to Fort Jesup, Louisiana. He left the Scotts at Fort Snelling, hiring them out to fellow officers. At Fort Jesup, he met and married Eliza Irene Sanford of St. Louis. Soon after his marriage, he sent for Dred and Harriet. The following year Emerson returned to Fort Snelling with his new wife and the Scotts. Thus Dred Scott had not only been taken into a state where slavery was illegal (Illinois), but he had now been taken twice into government territory where slavery was illegal.

Dred Scott Returns to St. Louis

Two years later, in 1840, Emerson traveled to Florida on what would be his last military assignment. Probably because of an ongoing Seminole war in the Florida Everglades, Emerson left his

THE NORTHWEST ORDINANCE AND
THE MISSOURI COMPROMISE

Sixty years before John Emerson took Dred Scott onto free soil, Congress passed the Northwest Ordinance, a measure establishing the guidelines by which territories could become states. The Ordinance limited slavery north of the Ohio River but allowed expansion of the practice to the south. Most important to Dred Scott's case, it contained a bill of rights that stated: "There shall be neither slavery nor involuntary servitude in said territory."

The United States maintained an equal number of slave states and free states until 1819. At that time Missouri applied for admission to the Union. Admitting Missouri as a slave state would upset the balance, and would also extend slavery beyond the line specified by the Northwest Ordinance.

A newspaper dated March 11, 1820, discusses the Missouri Compromise.

North and South divided on the issue. Southerners wanted Missouri admitted to the Union; Northerners did not. The agreement that was reached became known as the Missouri Compromise. Missouri was admitted to the Union as a slave state. Maine was admitted as a free state. Thus the number of slave and free states remained equal. Also, the Compromise, established a line west from Missouri dividing the lands that would be open to slavery from those that would not. And it "forever prohibited" slavery north of the Compromise line.

Thirty-six years later, the Missouri Compromise faced the judgment of the U. S. Supreme Court along with Dred Scott.

wife and the Scotts at her father's estate in St. Louis. It is unclear what the duties of Dred and Harriet were at that time, but most likely Irene Emerson would have either employed them for her personal use or hired them out as servants.

By this time, Dred and Harriet had an eighteen-month-old daughter, Eliza. After his long absence from St. Louis, Scott may have visited the Blow family to show off Eliza and to renew old ties. In later years, he described Taylor Blow as one of "them boys" he had been "raised" with, indicating he had a close relationship with the Blow children.

Lasting Ties

Indeed, despite his sale to Dr. Emerson, Dred Scott remained closely associated with the Blow family all his life. Henry Blow, who testified for Scott in circuit court, was fifteen years old when his parents died. And his brother Taylor was only twelve. Both brothers, especially the younger Taylor, later assisted Dred Scott throughout his long fight for freedom. It was Taylor who in 1867 had Dred Scott's body removed from an abandoned cemetery and reburied in a plot that was properly maintained.

The Blow family's loyalty to Scott is not clearly understood. It has not been put down to antislavery sentiment because most of the Blow family supported the South during the Civil War. Their kindness probably had its roots in childhood, especially in the case of Taylor Blow, whose loyalty to Scott never wavered. Pulitzer Prize–winning author Don Fehrenbacher writes in his book *The Dred Scott Case: Its Significance in American Law and Politics:* "Perhaps the sale [of Scott] distressed some of the younger children and especially the third son, Taylor. To a boy suddenly orphaned at the age of twelve, it may have meant the loss of a good friend at a bad time." The diminutive Dred Scott (scarcely five feet tall) must have possessed some admirable qualities to have inspired a young child to a lifetime of such affection and loyalty.

John Emerson's Last Will and Testament

Three years after Mrs. Emerson and the Scotts returned to St. Louis, Dr. Emerson died. He left his entire estate, including the Scott family, to his wife, Irene. He named a friend in Iowa and his wife's brother, John F. A. Sanford, as his executors. However, for reasons unknown the court appointed Irene Emerson's father as executor instead. John Sanford never participated in executing his brother-in-law's will, and there seems to be no connection between Emerson's will and John Sanford's later involvement in the Dred Scott trial.

The Long Fight for Freedom Begins

After John Emerson died, it appears that Mrs. Emerson loaned Dred Scott to her brother-in-law, Captain Bainbridge, for a period of two years. At least, Scott was known to be in Bainbridge's service at a military post in Texas in February 1846, when the captain sent him back to St. Louis, probably at Mrs. Emerson's request. In March, Mrs. Emerson hired Dred and Harriet out to a local man named Samuel Russell.

At that time Dred Scott asked Mrs. Emerson for permission to "hire his own time," that is, to find work for wages. Such work would enable him to save enough money to buy freedom for himself and his family. Slave owners in cities sometimes allowed favored slaves this privilege, so it was not an unusual appeal. However, according to Scott, Mrs. Emerson refused his request.

Dred and Harriet Scott decided to seek justice in the courts. On April 6, 1846, they petitioned Missouri's Circuit Court of St. Louis County for permission to sue for their freedom. The request was granted. On that same day, Francis B. Murdoch, the Scotts' attorney, filed two suits, one for each plaintiff, charging Irene Emerson with trespass and false imprisonment, the customary complaint in freedom cases. Claiming to be "free

After John Emerson's death, Dred Scott worked for Mrs. Emerson's brother-in-law, Captain William Bainbridge (pictured).

FIRST STEPS TO FREEDOM

A year before the Scotts petitioned for freedom, Missouri revised and published "An act to enable persons held in slavery to sue for their freedom." This law confirmed the right of a slave to sue for freedom. It also outlined the procedure to be followed and the special conditions to be met in such cases.

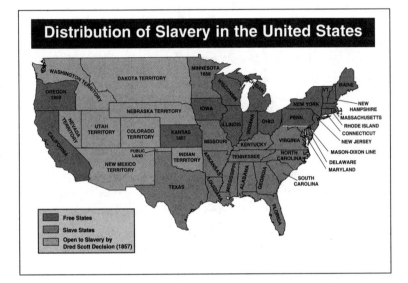

Distribution of Slavery in the United States

Free States
Slave States
Open to Slavery by
Dred Scott Decision (1857)

1. The slave must demonstrate "security [ability to pay] . . . for all costs that may be adjudged against him or her."

2. The slave must "have reasonable liberty to attend . . . the court [sessions]."

3. The slave was not to be "subject to any [punishment] on account of his application for freedom."

4. The slave was not to be "removed out of the jurisdiction of the court."

The law further stated that the suit should be "in the common form of a declaration for false imprisonment," with "a [declaration] that the plaintiff [slave] before and at the time of [filing] the grievances was, and still is, a free person, and that the defendant [owner] held, and still holds him in slavery." Dred and Harriet Scott followed these procedures when they filed suit against Mrs. Emerson for false imprisonment.

persons," both Dred and Harriet accused Mrs. Emerson of holding them as slaves, Dred Scott also charged her with assault, claiming that she had "beat, bruised and ill-treated" him and had temporarily imprisoned him.

So in the beginning, Mrs. Emerson faced two suits in the Missouri lower court: *Dred Scott v. Irene Emerson* and *Harriet Scott v. Irene Emerson*. Court proceedings in the two cases were essentially the same. In fact, four years later all parties agreed that "inasmuch as the points and principles of law to be decided [in the two cases] were identical," only *Dred Scott v. Irene Emerson* would continue through the courts. And the decision reached in Dred Scott's case would apply to Harriet's as well. (In truth they were not identical; unlike Dred, Harriet had not lived in Illinois for two years.)

Origin of *Dred Scott v. Irene Emerson*

Historians have long debated how the suits against Irene Emerson came about. What prompted two illiterate slaves to sue for their freedom? Was it their own idea or were the suits orchestrated by someone else for political reasons? Like so many things about Dred Scott, the exact circumstances are shrouded in mystery. However, it is not difficult to accept that Dred Scott himself came up with the idea of suing for freedom. Despite his illiteracy, he must have learned a great deal in his travels with Dr. Emerson. And Scott most certainly would have heard about slaves who had won freedom after their masters took them to live on free soil. He may also have sought advice from the Blow family.

Moreover, there is no evidence that the Dred Scott suit originated either for political reasons or out of someone's desire to make it a test case. Missouri courts had repeatedly freed slaves who had lived in a free state or free territory for an extended length of time. And the issues of slavery in the territories and the validity of the Missouri Compromise had not yet become a national political controversy.

Therefore, the suit seems to have begun for the simple reason that Dred Scott hungered for freedom for himself and his family. Later, when antislavery and proslavery advocates focused on slavery as a political issue, the Dred Scott case would assume

MYSTERY ATTORNEY

Francis B. Murdoch, Dred Scott's first attorney, filed the original court documents that charged Mrs. Emerson with trespass and false imprisonment. At the same time, he signed a bond accepting responsibility for any costs that might accrue in the case. Why he was willing to do this, and how he came to represent the Scotts in the first place, is a puzzle. Murdoch did have antislavery sympathies, but he was not a "slave lawyer."

One explanation is based on a chain of circumstances that could have connected Murdoch to the Scotts. Murdoch had been the prosecuting attorney in Alton, Illinois, when abolitionist and newspaper publisher Elijah P. Lovejoy was murdered by a rioting mob that was trying to destroy his printing press. Also living in Alton at the time was a Reverend John R. Anderson, who worked as a typesetter for Lovejoy. Later, Anderson moved to St. Louis and became pastor of the Second African Baptist Church—the church Harriet Scott attended. The lawyer Murdoch also moved from Alton to St. Louis after the Lovejoy case.

Thus the Scotts' lawyer and minister both came to St. Louis from the same small town, both had antislavery sympathies, and both had been involved in some way with the slain Lovejoy. These connected events suggest the possibility that Murdoch may have become involved with the Scotts through Reverend Anderson. To add to the mystery, Murdoch left St. Louis in 1847 before the case he had initiated came to trial.

a broader importance. But the original lawyers who assisted Scott appear to have had no other motives beyond a humanitarian desire to help a slave obtain freedom.

In any event, the suit was filed. And in view of the Missouri Supreme Court's previous decisions, it seemed certain that Dred and Harriet Scott would soon be free. But from the outset, the Scott suit moved through the court system at an agonizingly slow pace with endless delays and postponements. Seven months passed before Mrs. Emerson's attorneys filed her plea of not guilty. Then, due to a crowded court schedule, the suits did not come to trial until June 30, 1847, fourteen months after the Scotts filed their original petition.

This delay was unfortunate for the Scotts because the political climate in the United States had already begun to change. In 1846, only a month after Dred and Harriet Scott filed their court petitions, the United States went to war with Mexico to acquire California and the Oregon territory. The primary concern over this war for Mexican territory was its effect on slavery in the states. It was obvious that sooner or later new states would be created out of this vast new territory, which was not considered in the Missouri Compromise. Would the new states be slave or free? The carefully maintained balance between the number of slave states and the number of free states would again be in jeopardy.

Bitter arguments over the question of slavery in the new territories erupted in Congress. For the first time congressmen voted not according to party lines, but according to regional affiliation. By the time Dred Scott's case finally came to trial in 1847, the division between the American North and South had increased considerably.

First Trial, Scott Versus Emerson

Dred Scott v. Irene Emerson began on June 30, 1847, in the Circuit Court of St. Louis County; the presiding judge was Alexander Hamilton (not the revolutionary). George W. Goode, a Virginia lawyer with strong proslavery sentiments, represented Irene Emerson. By this time, the Blow family had stepped in to assume Scott's legal expenses. Samuel M. Bay, a former attorney general of Missouri, was hired to replace Francis Murdoch as Dred Scott's lawyer. How such a prestigious man came to represent Scott is not known. Professor Walter Ehrlich, in *They Have No Rights: Dred Scott's Struggle for Freedom*, notes that Bay served as an officer in a bank owned by a brother-in-law of the Blows. He speculates that Bay's hiring may have come out of that association. In any event, Bay took over Scott's case.

Case for the Plaintiff

Samuel Bay needed to prove only that Dred Scott had been taken to live in free territory, and that Irene Emerson was now holding him as her slave. Bay called as a witness, Henry Blow, who testified that his father had once owned Scott and had sold him to John Emerson. Bay also presented depositions (written testimony taken under oath) from soldiers who had known Emerson and Scott at Fort Snelling. But he relied primarily on the testimony of Samuel Russell. Russell swore that he had hired the Scotts from Irene Emerson and had made the necessary payment to her father. Other witnesses were present but Bay, confident that he had proved his case, did not call them.

Case for the Defense

Irene Emerson's attorney, George Goode, did not challenge either the depositions or the oral testimony of Henry Blow. However, he did question Samuel Russell. And on cross-examination Russell admitted that in fact he had not hired Dred Scott; rather, Adeline Russell, Samuel's wife, had made all the arrangements. Russell himself had only paid the hiring money to Mrs. Emerson's father. He "supposed that [the money] was for Mrs. Emerson, but he did not know it." Goode declared his case ready for the jury.

Technically Speaking

The cross-examination of Samuel Russell called into question his testimony for the plaintiff, Dred Scott. Should the testimony be allowed to stand? It was, after all, hearsay, because Mrs. Russell had actually hired the Scotts. Goode also noted in his closing argument that although Irene Emerson's father accepted money from the Russells, that did not make him Mrs. Emerson's agent. Dred Scott, Goode said, had not legally proved that it was specifically Mrs. Emerson who was holding him as a slave.

After the closing arguments, Judge Hamilton instructed the jury that Goode's statements were correct. Russell's testimony had not proved that Irene Emerson now owned Dred Scott. Nor should the jury assume that the defendant's father had acted as her agent. In other words, Scott had to prove that Irene Emerson owned him before he could win his freedom from her.

The First Verdict

Dred and Harriet Scott had waited over a year for their day in court. Now their case was heard and the verdict was returned in a single day. In view of the judge's instructions, the jury had no

In their first trial to petition for freedom, Dred and Harriet Scott remained slaves because of a technicality.

choice but to return a verdict in favor of the defendant, Irene Emerson. "The said defendant is not guilty in manner and form as the plaintiff hath in his declaration complained against her" was the jury's statement.

The verdict allowed Irene Emerson to keep Dred and Harriet Scott as her slaves even though, according to the court, there was no proof that they really were her slaves. Obviously, justice had failed Dred Scott because of a legal technicality, or a loophole in the law.

There was no public reaction to the verdict in St. Louis or elsewhere. The trial, after all, had not involved any unusual or controversial principles of law. Nor had it involved any well-known people. The case was special to no one except Dred and Harriet Scott, who had lost their chance for freedom.

However, the fight was far from over. Even before he left the courtroom, Samuel Bay, Dred Scott's attorney, began preparations for the next round.

Chapter 2

Up and Down the State Court Pyramid

On June 30, 1847, the same day the Missouri circuit court ruled that Dred Scott was still a slave, Samuel Bay moved for a new trial. He argued that Samuel Russell's testimony could be easily validated by calling Mrs. Russell as a witness. The judge agreed to consider a retrial.

Dred Scott's lawyer was determined to close all possible technical loopholes. He filed petitions to institute a new pair of suits for Dred and Harriet—this time against not only Irene Emerson but also her father and the witness, Samuel Russell. Scott's lawyer reasoned that surely one of these defendants would be found guilty of illegally holding the Scotts as slaves after they had become free under the Missouri Compromise. The court scheduled the new cases on its November docket.

However, a month later it dawned on the court that now Dred and Harriet Scott each had two cases pending, all four of which named Irene Emerson as a defendant. The Scotts were told they must choose one pair of suits or the other. They decided to proceed with the original suits naming only Irene Emerson.

The circuit court reassembled for its new term in November. By that time Dred Scott had two new lawyers, Alexander Field and David Hall. It is not clear exactly when Samuel Bay dropped out of the case. Court records indicate that the three lawyers worked together briefly, but within a few months Bay was no longer on the case.

First State Supreme Court Appeal

On December 2, the circuit court granted Dred Scott a new trial. But the next day Irene Emerson's lawyers filed an objection to the court's ruling. Such an objection meant the case would automatically be transferred to the Supreme Court of Missouri on a writ of error, a court order directing a higher court to review the judgment of a lower court. In what was fast becoming standard practice in the Scott case, proceedings were delayed. Because of a court clerical error, the circuit court trial transcript was not forwarded to the Missouri Supreme Court until March 6, 1848, four months later.

Meanwhile, Irene Emerson requested that the Scotts be taken into custody by the sheriff and hired out. Under this arrangement, she would not be directly responsible for the Scotts during litigation. This did not affect her claim on them, however, and whatever wages the Scotts earned would be paid to her. The court granted this request because Missouri law allowed for such arrangements in freedom cases.

One of the few photographs taken of Dred Scott.

By now the Scotts had a second daughter, probably born in 1847. They had named her Lizzie. Lizzie's future, as well as that of her sister, Eliza, would also be determined by the outcome of her father's case.

Circuit Court Ruling Upheld

The Missouri Supreme Court heard the *Dred Scott v. Irene Emerson* appeal on April 3, 1848. The matter to be decided was not Dred Scott's

UNDERSTANDING THE COURT SYSTEM

The U. S. court system comprises two parts: the state courts and the federal courts. The two courts operate alongside, but independently of, each other. Both are structured in the form of a pyramid with the supreme or highest court of each at the top.

The federal courts can hear only those cases designated by the Constitution, that is, lawsuits against the U.S. government, cases involving the constitutionality of a federal law, and lawsuits between citizens from different states. The state courts hear all cases that do not involve the federal government.

At the time of the Dred Scott trial, the Missouri state courts consisted of a circuit court, where lawsuits were initiated, and the Missouri Supreme Court, for appeals. The composition of the federal courts was similar, with a district court in which lawsuits were initiated, and the U.S. Supreme Court for appeals.

Dred Scott's suit began in, and moved through, the state courts. His lawyers then filed a new suit in federal court, which led Scott to the U.S. Supreme Court, the country's highest court.

---

freedom, but whether the lower court had erred in granting Scott a new trial. Both sides presented their arguments in written briefs (documents citing points of law) rather than in oral statements.

Irene Emerson's attorney, George Goode, maintained that the lower court had erred because Dred Scott's counsel had failed to prove that Mrs. Emerson was "in any manner connected with his being held in slavery." Again Goode did not dispute Scott's residence in free territory, but relied solely on the legal technicality to win the appeal.

However, Scott's lawyers, Field and Hall, also knew how to capitalize on technicalities. They argued that a writ of error for an appeal cannot be issued until after a lower court has made a final judgment. Because the new trial ordered by the lower court had not yet taken place, no final judgment had been made. Therefore, it was improper for the Missouri Supreme Court to consider the appeal.

On June 30, the Missouri Supreme Court justices agreed with Scott's lawyers. They dismissed the writ of error and let the lower court's ruling for a new trial stand. Dred Scott was assured of a second chance. His suit for freedom would be retried in the lower circuit court.

While Dred Scott Waited

Dred Scott had won the right to a retrial, but another year and a half would pass before the new trial took place. A combination of circumstances caused the delay; twice it was rescheduled to relieve the court's case overload. Finally it was scheduled for late May 1849. But on May 17 a fire that broke out on the St. Louis waterfront spread through the city, destroying homes and businesses. Around the same time, the city suffered a cholera epidemic. All court cases were suspended until the crises passed.

At some point during this wait for a retrial, Irene Emerson left St. Louis and moved to Springfield, Massachusetts. She turned the supervision of her business affairs—including the Dred Scott trial—over to her brother, John Sanford. Sanford discharged attorney George Goode from the case. In his place, he hired Hugh Garland, a respected attorney and former member of the Virginia legislature, and his partner, Lyman D. Norris.

For the Supreme Court appeal, John Sanford replaced George Goode with attorney Hugh Garland (pictured).

Second State Circuit Court Trial

The long-awaited retrial began at last on January 12, 1850. The second trial progressed much the same as the first. Once again Scott's lawyers, Field and Hall, established that Scott had been taken into free territory and then brought back to Missouri and held illegally as a slave. The depositions used in the first trial were again presented to the court. However, Field and Hall introduced a new deposition by Adeline Russell. Mrs. Russell swore that she had hired the Scotts from Irene Emerson, and that Mrs. Emerson had claimed she owned them. Mrs. Russell said also that the transaction had taken place between herself and Mrs. Emerson personally. Samuel Russell testified again that he had paid the Scotts' wages. Counsel for Dred Scott then rested their case.

Case for the Defendant

Irene Emerson's attorneys neither called nor cross-examined a single witness. Considering Mrs. Russell's sworn testimony, they could no longer argue lack of proof that Mrs. Emerson had been the one to hire Dred Scott out to the Russells. Abandoning their original defense, Garland and Norris switched tactics and insisted that Mrs. Emerson had a right to hire Scott out because he was still her slave regardless of his travels with Dr. Emerson. They argued that while Scott resided on free soil he had been subject to military and not civil law. They were careful, however, not to mention the case of *Rachel v. Walker*, in which a slave named Rachel had been freed despite that same military law argument.

Rachel v. Walker tried in the courts in 1836, was an example of the numerous cases in which slaves sued for freedom in the Missouri courts and won. Rachel was the slave of an army officer. She had accompanied the officer from St. Louis to Fort Snelling in Wisconsin free territory—the same army post where Dred Scott later served Dr. Emerson. After returning to St. Louis, she sued for her freedom. The court decided in her favor, noting that she had been required to stay at those posts.

The court declared also that "an officer of the U. S. Army who takes his slave to a military post, within the territory wherein slavery is prohibited, and retains her several years in attendance on himself and family, forfeits his property in such slave by virtue of the [Northwest] ordinance of 1787." The similarity of *Rachel v. Walker* to the Dred Scott case was unmistakable, but Scott's lawyers had not needed to cite it.

The Second Verdict

The jury found the defendant, Irene Emerson, "guilty of manner and form as in the plaintiff's declaration alleged." After four

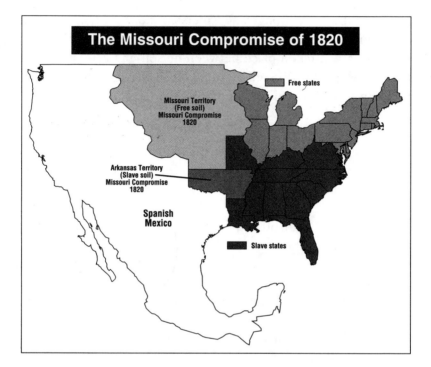

The Missouri Compromise of 1820

Free states

Missouri Territory
(Free soil)
Missouri Compromise
1820

Arkansas Territory
(Slave soil)
Missouri Compromise
1820

Spanish
Mexico

Slave states

years in the courts, Dred Scott was free and so were his wife and daughters. But the victory was short-lived.

Emerson's lawyers immediately moved for a new trial. When their motion was denied, the defense attorneys took the necessary steps for an appeal to the Missouri Supreme Court. Their intention is difficult to fathom; since the circuit court's ruling was consistent with innumerable Missouri Supreme Court precedents—in which slaves who had resided in free states were declared to be free—the chance of winning such an appeal was unlikely.

Equally baffling is the question of why Irene Emerson was so determined to pursue the case. Historians have speculated that ill feeling might have developed between the Blow family, who was paying Dred Scott's court costs, and the Emerson-Sanford family. Others have suggested that when Mrs. Emerson left St. Louis, she may have sold the Scotts to her brother, John Sanford. In that case Sanford, a shrewd businessman, might have been reluctant to lose property and money without putting up a fight.

No evidence exists to support either of these suppositions.

But whatever the motivation, the Dred Scott case would make a return appearance before the Missouri Supreme Court.

Second Missouri Supreme Court Appeal

Attorneys for both sides filed their briefs in the Missouri Supreme Court on March 8, 1850. Garland, who filed for Mrs. Emerson, argued that Dr. Emerson had gone into free territory only because as an army officer, he was "subject to the order and direction of the Government, whose servant he was." He had not "voluntarily and of his own free will" gone into free territory. Therefore, he could not "voluntarily and of his own free will" have taken Dred Scott there with him. He had had no other choice.

Garland's second argument—a repeat of his argument in the lower court—was that military rather than civil law had applied to Emerson. He did not claim that the Northwest Ordinance and the Missouri Compromise were unconstitutional. But he held that they were both civil laws and that when a conflict existed between civil law and military law, military law should prevail.

David Hall filed the brief for Dred Scott. He restated his circuit court argument that, according to Missouri law, Scott was entitled to freedom because of his residence on free soil. Then he addressed Garland's military law versus civil law argument. He noted that *Rachel v. Walker* had already established that it made no difference whether a slave taken into free territory was on military or civilian property. He admitted that a soldier had no choice but to go wherever the army sent him. However, he pointed out that when

Attorney Hugh Garland argued that Dred Scott was still a slave on the grounds that military, not civil law, should govern Scott's status.

STRADER V. GRAHAM

As the Scott-Emerson briefs were being filed in the Missouri Supreme Court, the U. S. Supreme Court prepared to rule on another case. *Strader v. Graham* did not involve a slave suing for freedom. It was a suit brought by a slave owner against a man he accused of helping his slaves escape. Christopher Graham of Kentucky owned three slaves who were musicians. He had allowed them to travel into Indiana and Ohio (free states) to perform. One day they boarded a steamboat owned by Jacob Strader of Ohio, traveled with him to Cincinnati, and disappeared.

Graham sued Strader for the value of the slaves and won. Strader appealed to the Supreme Court, arguing that the slaves had been free men when they boarded his boat, having become free under the laws of Indiana and Ohio and the Northwest Ordinance.

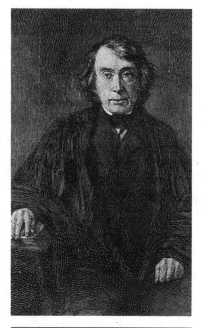

Chief Justice Roger Taney

The Supreme Court ruled that it did not have jurisdiction to try the case. The status of the slaves, free or enslaved, at the time of their flight, the Court said, must be decided by the courts of Kentucky. In a preview of the Dred Scott decision, Chief Justice Roger Taney, after announcing the Court's verdict, went on to endorse the Kentucky court's decision. The Kentucky court had ruled that even if the slaves had been free while they were in Ohio, once they returned to Kentucky their status depended on Kentucky's laws. Taney stated further that the Northwest Ordinance was no longer effective in Indiana and Ohio because they were now states, not territories.

In the Missouri Supreme Court two years later, Irene Emerson's lawyers made productive use of *Strader v. Graham*, especially Taney's appended remarks.

Emerson left Scott in the free state of Illinois, hired out as a slave to others, he did so voluntarily. Scott was therefore entitled to his freedom and the decision of the lower court should stand.

Although both briefs were filed on schedule, a heavy caseload prevented Dred Scott's case from being heard during the March term. Regrettably for Dred Scott, it was only the first of many postponements. It would be two years almost to the day before the Missouri Supreme Court rendered a verdict on whether or not to uphold the lower court's ruling to free Dred Scott. By that time, dramatic events had occurred throughout the nation, events that would influence the Missouri court and bring national politics into the courtroom.

While Dred Scott Waited

During the two years Scott waited for the court's decision, bitter arguments over whether to allow slavery in the territories increased slaveholding states' resistance to suits for freedom. And in the North, the Fugitive Slave Act stirred up more hostility against slavery than any prior legislation.

In 1850, U.S. president Zachary Taylor—without consulting Congress—advised California and New Mexico to draw up constitutions and request admission to the Union. In response, the two territories wrote constitutions that banned slavery. Southern extremists threatened secession from the Union because if California and New Mexico were admitted as free states, it would upset the balance in the Senate between free and slave states. In an effort to save the Union, Congress passed a series of bills that became known as the Compromise of 1850. This Compromise allowed California to enter the Union as a free state. However, Utah and New Mexico were formed as new territories with the slavery question left open for their own voters to decide. Texas received $10 million in return for giving up all claim to the New Mexico Territory. The Compromise eased tension between the North and South in some ways, but it increased the sectional hostility in other ways.

A controversial part of the Compromise was the Fugitive Slave Act, which denied runaway slaves a jury trial and prevented them from testifying in their own behalf. It also compelled northern citizens to help enforce the act by returning runaway slaves to their masters.

Then in 1852, publication of Harriet Beecher Stowe's antislavery novel *Uncle Tom's Cabin* added to the growing furor. Its impact on northerners made enforcement of the Fugitive Slave Act extremely difficult. And the book enraged southerners and southern sympathizers. With each new controversy, the Missouri courts became more hostile to cases that involved granting freedom to slaves. And Dred Scott's chances of becoming a free man diminished proportionately.

Chapter 3

Return to Slavery

MISSOURI, SURROUNDED ON THREE SIDES by free territory, was especially sensitive to the escalating tension over slavery. And it was in the Missouri Supreme Court that politics first entered the Dred Scott case.

The Missouri Supreme Court comprised three justices, or judges. Two of the three were proslavery. By August 1851 those two had already decided to reject Scott's bid for freedom in order to challenge the Missouri Compromise. However, their decision was delayed while the makeup of the court was reshuffled.

In an election of judges for Missouri courts, two of the Supreme Court justices, including the sole abolitionist, were voted out and replaced with new ones. Hamilton R. Gamble, one of the newly elected justices, was an antislavery advocate. But that would not help Dred Scott because the other two, both proslavery, had the majority vote.

When the new court convened on October 20, 1851, Dred Scott's case was almost postponed again. However, at the last minute his lawyer managed to get it on the court calender. (Alexander Field was now Scott's sole lawyer, David Hall having died.) Field submitted to the court the same briefs that both sides had filed in 1850.

New Arguments

Meanwhile, one of Irene Emerson's attorneys, Lyman Norris, was working on a supplemental brief that presented new arguments. Before he completed it, the case was turned over to Justice William Scott (no relation to Dred) to write the state high court's opinion.

An engraving graphically depicts the effects of the Fugitive Slave law—slaves are brutally hunted down as they try to escape to the North.

William Scott, the second newly elected justice, was an avid proponent of slavery. That he had been chosen to write the opinion practically guaranteed that the verdict would be in favor of Irene Emerson. Lyman Norris, therefore, had no real need to submit the new arguments. Nevertheless, he hurriedly obtained permission to file the additional, unfinished brief.

The contents of the new brief revealed why Norris had been so eager to submit it to the court. It expressed the ever-increasing belief among southerners that the North meant to destroy the South's way of life by continuing to prohibit slavery in the territories. In his statement, Norris denounced the authority of both the Northwest Ordinance and the Missouri Compromise. He did not go so far as to challenge their constitutionality, but he argued that any laws based upon them could not be enforced. Quoting from an earlier U. S. Supreme Court decision in *Strader v. Graham*, Norris used Chief Justice Roger Brooke Taney's argument that the Northwest Ordinance no longer applied.

That being the case, Norris said, the legal precedents quoted by Dred Scott's attorneys were based upon "false legal principles" and should be reversed. It seems clear that Norris filed the new brief not to help his client, Irene Emerson, but to make a political statement.

Norris ended his brief with a racist statement about the dangers of encouraging "the multiplication of a race whose condition could be neither that of [all] freemen or [all] slaves." Such circumstances, he said, "tends only to dissatisfy and corrupt those . . . remaining in a State of Servitude [enslavement]."

Historian Walter Ehrlich, commenting on Norris's statement, writes:

> What had started as a routine freedom case had now stirred up two explosive issues that already were plaguing the nation and that were to become even more important later: the political status of slavery and the attitudes of white America toward blacks. . . . What Norris injected into the case was . . . the undisguised . . . argument that blacks were inferior to whites.

Once again the court term ended before a verdict could be announced.

The Third Verdict

The court reconvened in March 1852. In a two-to-one vote, the Missouri Supreme Court ruled that Dred Scott was still a slave, and ordered that the judgment of the lower court—which had granted Scott his freedom—be reversed.

Justice William Scott then read the opinion of the court, which elaborated on the verdict. He acknowledged that in numerous Missouri cases similar to Dred Scott's, slaves had been granted freedom because of residence in free territory. But those decisions, said Justice Scott, were based on the grounds that Missouri courts were bound to enforce the laws of other states, "regardless of the rights . . . or the institutions of the people of [Missouri]."

He went on to say that Missouri courts had no obligation to recognize the laws of other states when they conflicted with Missouri laws:

Every state has the right of determining how far in a spirit of comity [cooperation] it will respect the laws of other States. Those laws have no intrinsic [built-in] right to be enforced beyond the limits of the State for which they were enacted. The respect allowed them will depend altogether on their conformity to the policy of [Missouri] institutions. No state is bound to carry into effect enactments conceived in a spirit hostile to that which pervades her own laws.

OPINION OF THE COURT

When Judge William Scott—after announcing the Missouri Supreme Court's verdict—read the opinion of the court, he was speaking obiter dictum. This Latin phrase means a statement made by a judge in connection with a verdict he is rendering. Literally, it means "a statement made in passing." It has no legal bearing on the court's ruling, but it may have considerable influence on later cases. In some cases, as in the *Strader v. Graham* ruling, the opinion may become more important than the ruling itself.

John Marshall, chief justice of the Supreme Court from 1801 to 1835, invented the opinion of the Court procedure. It remains in use today just as he established it. One justice is chosen to write the opinion of the Court and any justice who is outvoted can write a dissenting opinion explaining why he or she disagrees. Before Marshall, there was no way to determine by what reasoning the Court reached a particular decision. Therefore, when William Scott elaborated on the Missouri Supreme Court's ruling, he was following a well-established precedent.

Chief Justice John Marshall devised the way in which Supreme Court opinions are handed down today— with both a majority opinion and dissenting opinions being written.

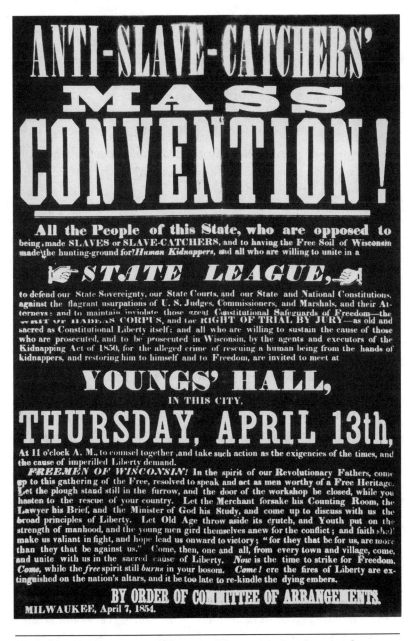

An 1854 antislavery poster. Wisconsin did not recognize slaves as the property of other states.

In a statement that demonstrates how politics had influenced the court, Justice Scott then declared: "Times are not now as they were when the former decisions on this subject were made. Since then not only individuals but States have been possessed with a dark . . . spirit in relation to slavery."

Dissenting Opinion

The antislavery justice, Hamilton R. Gamble, also aware of the changing times, wrote a dissenting opinion. He began with this statement: "The questions involved in the case, and the present condition of feeling in the country, seem to require that I should state the grounds of [my] dissent."

Justice Gamble's dissent dealt primarily with the legal principle of stare decisis, or the argument that the court should be guided by the precedents of earlier decisions. He did not disagree outright with Justice Scott's opinion that Missouri could choose whether to uphold another state's laws. Instead, he argued that Missouri courts had already made that choice by upholding the laws of other states in earlier rulings.

Justice Gamble cited many precedents that demonstrated cooperation between states. He recounted cases from other states as well as those of Missouri. In all such rulings, he pointed out, it was either explicitly stated or implied that "where a right to freedom has been acquired under the law of another State . . . , it may be enforced by action in the Courts of a slaveholding State."

To further support his argument, Gamble added that those earlier cases had been decided "when the public mind was tranquil." "Times," Gamble said, "may have changed, public feeling may have changed, but principles have not and do not change."

But the Missouri Supreme Court had rendered its decision. According to Don E. Fehrenbacher in *The Dred Scott Case*, the court's ruling was "primarily an expression of mounting southern anger and an act of retaliation against antislavery words and deeds." Therefore, the Missouri court—with its majority of proslavery justices—had welcomed reviewing the Dred Scott case. But although the court's ruling on March 22, 1852, ended *Dred Scott v. Irene Emerson*, it did not end the Dred Scott case.

Yet twenty-two months would pass before any further action was taken to continue Dred Scott's fight for legal freedom. Immediately after the Missouri Supreme Court's ruling, Irene Emerson requested that the Scotts be released from the sheriff's custody and returned to her, along with all the money they had earned since she hired them out in 1848. This was a routine request in such cases, but surprisingly, and for reasons not clear, the judge refused to grant it. The court's record notes only, "Said motion be overruled." The judge may have had some private knowledge that the Scott forces planned to continue the case, but that seems unlikely, as almost a year and a half passed before a new suit was initiated.

No surviving records document the daily activities of Dred Scott and his wife and daughters during this period. However, records do show what was happening *to* him. Between June 1852 and November 1853, he acquired a new lawyer, allegedly got a new owner, and his new lawyer decided to take the case to the federal courts.

From State Court to Federal Court

As is so often the case in Dred Scott's story, many events that followed this latest verdict are clouded by uncertainty. But one undisputed fact is that Alexander Field moved to Louisiana and could no longer represent Scott. If Dred Scott's case were to continue, he needed a new lawyer.

Charles LaBeaume was a brother-in-law of Henry Blow, a son of Dred Scott's original owner. LaBeaume was also a lawyer. He had been a benefactor of Dred Scott's since the case began back in 1846. Two years after Irene Emerson had Scott placed in the custody of the St. Louis County sheriff, LaBeaume hired Scott from the sheriff. As far as is known, Scott remained in his employment throughout the litigation. Now LaBeaume approached Roswell M. Field (no relation to Alexander Field) and asked him to take over Dred Scott's case. Field, an abolitionist lawyer with a considerable reputation, accepted the challenge.

If Roswell Field had followed standard procedure, he would have appealed the Missouri Supreme Court's decision directly to the U.S. Supreme Court. But he believed such an appeal would be doomed to failure, because at the time the only grounds for appeal were that a state court had erred in its decision. And on those grounds, Chief Justice Roger Taney would undoubtedly refuse to review the case, just as he had done in *Strader v. Graham*.

Field decided that instead of appealing he would initiate a new suit—this time in the federal courts. He could not bring suit against Irene Emerson (now Mrs. Calvin Chaffee) because the two-year statute of limitations had expired. Also, by this time Irene Emerson Chaffee no longer had any active involvement with Scott's case. She had moved to Massachusetts and left her brother, John Sanford, to handle her business affairs. Whether she sold Scott to Sanford or whether Sanford was acting as her agent has never been determined. But the question of who owned Dred Scott does not appear to have been an issue. Everyone, including the courts, assumed that since Sanford had been named as executor in Dr. Emerson's will, he had some sort of legal connection to the Scotts.

By this time John Sanford had moved to New York. He had hired an agent to attend to his St. Louis business interests, which presumably included the Scotts. Roswell Field recognized this situation as a way of getting Dred Scott's case into the federal courts without coming up against the *Strader v. Graham* precedent. Under the law, suits between citizens of different states are tried in the federal courts. Accordingly, on November 2, 1853, suit was filed in U. S. circuit court against John F. A. Sanford.

*Dred Scott v. John F. A. Sandford**

The new suit claimed that Dred Scott, a citizen of Missouri, and his family were being illegally held as slaves by John Sanford, a citizen of New York. On the day of the filing, Charles LaBeaume and Taylor Blow bonded themselves to cover "all the costs and fees which may accrue by reason of the prosecution of the said suit."

The federal circuit court convened in St. Louis on April 3, 1854, with Judge Robert W. Wells presiding. Historian Don Fehrenbacher describes Wells as "a slaveholder who nevertheless regarded slavery as a barrier to progress [and who] was ap-

*A court reporter misspelled Sanford's name, and the error was never corrected.

WHO OWNED DRED SCOTT IN 1853?

On November 21, 1850, Irene Emerson married Calvin Clifford Chaffee, a physician in Springfield, Massachusetts. Oddly enough, Dr. Chaffee was a member of the antislavery Republican Party and would later be elected to Congress. Did Irene Emerson sell Dred Scott to her brother, John Sanford, when she remarried? Sanford's later testimony gives the impression that she did.

During the federal trial of *Dred Scott v. John F. A. Sandford* in 1853, John Sanford declared repeatedly that the Scotts were his "lawful property." On the other hand, no bill of sale has ever been found that shows they were sold to Sanford. And when John Sanford died in 1857, his estate made no mention of the Scotts. Moreover, three weeks after Sanford's death Taylor Blow bought the Scotts, not from Sanford's estate but from the Chaffees.

Yet if John Sanford did not own the Scotts, why did he allow himself to be sued as their owner? Don Fehrenbacher, in *The Dred Scott Case*, states that "the best explanation may be simply that [none of the people involved] knew for sure who owned the Scotts." But Fehrenbacher also notes the possibility that Sanford had acquired the Scotts from his sister in an informal way, or that acting as her agent, he allowed himself to be sued as if he were the owner.

Because of the many contradictions and lack of records, it is impossible to determine who actually owned Dred Scott at that time. It is doubtful that Dred Scott himself knew—or cared. All he wanted was his freedom.

---

parently free of the intense prejudice that had permeated the decision of the Missouri Supreme Court."

Before the trial began, John Sanford and his lawyer Hugh Garland filed a plea claiming that the court had no jurisdiction or right to hear the case because Dred Scott was not a citizen of Missouri. Sanford said Scott was not a citizen "because he is a negro of African descent—his ancestors were of pure African blood and were brought into this country and sold as negro slaves."

Roswell Field challenged Garland's plea, and both attorneys then presented arguments and cited precedents to support their positions. After listening to the arguments, Judge Wells rejected Sanford's plea. He ruled that Dred Scott had the right to sue, because citizenship implied nothing more than residence in a particular state and the legal right to own property.

In so ruling, Wells was going against the views held by slave states. Furthermore, he pointed out that if a free Negro did not have the right to sue, then neither could he be sued, and that would give him rights that free white citizens did not have. On this point Wells was assuming that Scott was free until proved otherwise. And strangely enough, Sanford's lawyers did not challenge this ruling. They could have argued that Scott was still a slave, and slaves could not bring suit in a federal court.

Instead, John Sanford, his original plea having been rejected, entered a new plea. He pleaded not guilty to Scott's charges. He had, he said, "gently laid his hands upon them [the Scotts] and restrained them of their liberty as he had a right to do."

However, the issue of black citizenship was now a part of the court record, and it would not go away. Walter Ehrlich writes:

> The citizenship of blacks . . . would become a major issue—made so not by the parties to the case, but by the Supreme Court itself. Neither side would say much about citizenship in arguments before the Supreme Court because neither side considered it that important to the case; their major concern was the permanence of freedom attained under the Ordinance of 1787. But the Supreme Court's first consideration . . . had to be jurisdiction—and the citizenship issue, considered at first a subsidiary matter, became paramount. Indeed, one of the main reasons the Supreme Court would order a second argument was so counsel could clarify points of law about citizenship.

Meanwhile in the federal circuit court—with the issue temporarily settled according to Judge Wells's ruling—the two sides proceeded to agree on a statement of facts for presentation to the court. And the case went to trial on May 15, 1854. The only evidence presented was the statement of facts that Roswell Field read to the jury. No witnesses were called and no new evidence was introduced. Field asked the judge to instruct the jury that Dred Scott should go free according to the provisions of the Northwest Ordinance, the constitution of Illinois, and the Missouri Compromise.

However, Judge Wells refused Field's request. Instead he instructed the jury that the law was with Sanford, the defendant. Agreeing with the Missouri Supreme Court, Wells said that Dred Scott was subject to the laws of Missouri, not Illinois. He stated later that he wished the law had been on Scott's side because he was "deeply interested in favor of the poor fellow." But Wells said he had had no other choice. "The U. S. Courts follow the State courts in regard to the interpretation of [a state's] own law," he declared. "I was bound to take the interpretation of the laws of Missouri in this case, from the Supreme Court of [that] State."

The jury found Sanford not guilty as charged. Dred Scott was still a slave. Roswell Field moved immediately for a new trial, but Judge Wells refused to grant the motion. Field then instituted an appeal to the Supreme Court of the United States.

Chapter 4

Dred Scott in the Supreme Court

B EYOND A ROUTINE PRINTING of court decisions, most St. Louis newspapers paid no attention to Dred Scott's appeal to the U. S. Supreme Court. Only the antislavery *St. Louis Daily Morning Herald* printed a brief summary that concluded: "Dred is, of course, poor and without any powerful friends. But no doubt he will find at the bar of the Supreme Court some able and generous advocate who will do all he can to establish his right to go free."

However, certain of the country's proslavery supporters had recognized the importance of the Dred Scott case. Alarmed by its potential political implications, when John Sanford's attorney died, an unidentified "southern gentleman" asked attorney Reverdy Johnson to defend Sanford before the Supreme Court.

Reverdy Johnson, a former senator from Maryland and U. S. attorney general under Zachary Taylor, was one of the country's most esteemed lawyers, especially in constitutional law. He agreed to take the case, but refused a fee. And Senator Henry S. Geyer of Missouri, also an attorney, volunteered his services on behalf of Sanford. John Sanford and the slaveholding South now had two of the best legal minds in the country representing them. But who would represent the slave Dred Scott?

Looking for an Advocate

Dred Scott's lawyer, Roswell Field, had no experience arguing cases before the Supreme Court. So after filing Scott's appeal

Reverdy Johnson, former senator of Maryland, was asked to defend John
Sanford before the Supreme Court in the Dred Scott appeal.

Field began searching for a qualified attorney to represent Scott
in the nation's highest court. He also had to raise money to pay
that attorney and to pay Scott's court fees. To that end, Charles
LaBeaume, the Blow family's brother-in-law, published a twelve-
page pamphlet describing the proceedings and outcome of the
most recent trial. An emotional preface to this summary (dated
July 4 for effect) was constructed as though Scott himself had
written it. Signed with Dred Scott's mark, it closed with a mov-
ing appeal for help:

> I have no money to pay anybody at Washington to speak
> for me. My fellow-countrymen, can any of you help me in
> my day of trial? Will nobody speak for me at Washington,

even without hope of other reward than the blessings of a poor black man and his family? I can only pray that some good heart will be moved by pity to do that for me which I can not do for myself; and that if the right is on my side, it may be so declared by the high court to which I have appealed.

Although the pamphlet was widely distributed among antislavery supporters, it evoked little response. This lethargy on the part of the normally zealous antislavery faction is hard to understand. Perhaps abolitionists were simply busy elsewhere, or perhaps they did not yet fully comprehend the significance of the Dred Scott case.

Serving the Cause of Humanity

In the meantime Roscoe Field had been trying to convince Montgomery Blair, an eminent Washington lawyer, to represent Scott before the Supreme Court. Field had first approached Blair in May, soon after the lower federal court's decision. But at that time Blair had been occupied elsewhere. On Christmas Eve 1854, Field again contacted Blair about taking the case. Field explained that neither Scott nor Scott's friends could afford to pay Blair for his services. He continued:

A year ago, I was employed to bring suit for Scott. The question is . . . whether the removal by the master of his slave to Illinois or Wisconsin, works an absolute emancipation. . . . If you . . . should feel interest enough in the case as to bring it to a hearing and decision by the Court, the cause of humanity may perhaps be [served], and at all events, a much disputed question would be settled by the highest Court of the Nation.

After consulting with family and friends, Montgomery Blair agreed to take the case without pay if someone would pay court expenses. Gamaliel Bailey, editor of the antislavery newspaper *National Era* and publisher of Harriet Beecher Stowe's novel *Uncle Tom's Cabin*, volunteered to pay court costs and incidental expenses.

Washington attorney Montgomery Blair agreed to defend Dred Scott before the Supreme Court.

Attorney for a Slave

Montgomery Blair—who in 1861 would be appointed postmaster general by Abraham Lincoln—was a good choice. An able and skilled lawyer, he was experienced in arguing cases before the U. S. Supreme Court. He had grown up in Missouri and had practiced law and served as judge of the court of common pleas there. This was a definite plus, as familiarity with Missouri law was crucial to understanding Scott's case.

But despite his abilities, Blair may have been overmatched by Sanford's formidable team of Geyer and Johnson. Blair was not unaware of this. In an interview with the *National Intelligencer* in December 1856 he stated: "I felt it my duty to seek assistance, especially . . . when I found arrayed against me the . . . [top] men of the [legal] profession of the East and the West."

However, it was late in the trial before Blair convinced another attorney to join him. In that same interview he explained why. The year 1856 was a presidential election year, and lawyers—whether they supported the antislavery or the proslavery cause—understood the potential explosiveness of the Supreme Court's decision. Consequently, Blair stated, they "were unwilling . . . to add to embarrassment of the cause [they supported] or that of the party with which they stood connected, by implicating either themselves or [their party] by [participating] in the result."

A DREAM DEFERRED

The following poem, from Langston Hughes's *Montage of a Dream Deferred*, written almost a century after Dred Scott died, describes the happy-on-the-outside image that blacks felt they must present in order to survive in a white society. Was Dred Scott, like the person in the poem, afraid to show his sadness about his "dream deferred"?

Dream Boogie

Good morning, daddy!
Ain't you heard
The boogie-woogie rumble
Of a dream deferred?

Listen closely:
You'll hear their feet
Beating out and beating out a—

*You think
It's a happy beat?*

Listen to it closely:
Ain't you heard
something underneath
like a—

What did I say?

Sure,
I'm happy!
Take it away!

*Hey, pop!
Re-bop!
Mop!*

        Y-e-a-h!

Dred Scott's Last Chance for Freedom

On December 30, 1854—the same day that Montgomery Blair informed Field he would accept the case—*Dred Scott v. John F. A. Sandford* (with Sanford's name still misspelled) was officially filed with the U. S. Supreme Court. It had been almost six months since the appeal was first requested. During that period Congress passed the Kansas-Nebraska Act, which repealed the part of the Missouri Compromise that banned slavery from the Kansas and Nebraska territories. Passage of this act virtually assured a civil war. Antislavery senator Charles Sumner said of this law: "It annuls all past compromises with slavery, and makes all future compromises impossible."

And another thirteen months would go by before the Supreme Court heard the first arguments. Historian Walter Ehrlich maintains that the delay was not intentional, but that "the [schedule] was just extremely crowded, and the Court simply did not reach the case until February 1856."

Political Views Color Decisions

In early February, when it became apparent that the Supreme Court would soon review the case, Montgomery Blair filed a written brief for Dred Scott. In the brief, he dealt first with the Missouri Supreme Court's ruling that when a freed person returned to a slave state, the person became enslaved again.

Blair argued that the state court had allowed current political views to influence its decision. He cited prior cases in which the U. S. Supreme Court had repeatedly recognized the common law principle that "liberty, once admitted, cannot be recalled." He claimed freedom for Scott only on the grounds of his residence in Illinois. For reasons known only to Blair, he did not mention Scott's stay at Fort Snelling. This omission may have been calculated to avoid the issue of slavery in the territories.

In the remainder of the brief, Blair addressed the question of whether a freed Negro was a citizen of the United States. Since the lower court's ruling on Negro citizenship had been in Scott's favor, it seems odd that Blair would call it to the Court's attention. Bringing up this issue would not help Dred Scott, and the point might never have been raised if Blair had not introduced it. Fehrenbacher suggests that Blair may have been influenced by Scott's Missouri lawyer, Roscoe Field, who had indicated he would like the Supreme Court to rule on that issue:

Blair, although not an abolitionist, was apparently enough of an antislavery man to virtually invite such [a ruling] in his brief, a course of action that could scarcely benefit his client. Dred Scott, out of sight back in St. Louis, was becoming more clearly a pawn in the political game.

Only Montgomery Blair appears to have submitted a written statement to the Court. There is no evidence that either Henry S. Geyer or Reverdy Johnson filed a brief for John Sanford, the defendant.

First Arguments

On Monday, February 11, 1856, the U. S. Supreme Court heard opening arguments in *Dred Scott v. John F. A. Sandford*. The presentations of the two sides extended over a period of four days. Unfortunately, no record exists of what was said; newspaper re-

The courtroom of the U. S. Supreme Court, where Dred Scott's appeal was heard.

HOW THE U. S. SUPREME COURT WORKS

The highest court in America reviews only a tiny percentage of the cases it receives. To reach the Supreme Court, cases must involve principles of law or constitutional issues of far-reaching importance. For example, when a law—new or old—is challenged, the Supreme Court decides whether or not that law violates the Constitution.

The U. S. Supreme Court was originally composed of one chief justice and five associate justices. But as the number of new states increased, more justices were added. By the time of Dred Scott's trial, the total had reached nine justices, the number sitting on today's Supreme Court.

No juries hear U. S. Supreme Court cases. No witnesses are called. Instead, lawyers for both sides submit written arguments, called briefs. The justices study these briefs along with the records from the lower court. Then a lawyer from each side presents an oral argument to the Court, during which the justices may interrupt at any time to ask questions.

The justices then consult together, each stating his or her opinion. Only the justices are present during these discussions. As in Dred Scott's case, they may hold several consultations before they take a preliminary vote. It is not necessary that they all agree. The majority opinion of five of the nine justices becomes the official decision. Once the U. S. Supreme Court rules, the decision can be overturned only by a constitutional amendment or a subsequent reversal by the Court itself in another case.

porters heard the arguments, but they printed only the highlights. It can be assumed that Blair's argument covered the points he had presented in his written brief. Newspaper reports indicate that Sanford's lawyers used the same arguments they had used in the lower court. Those would have included the contention that the case should not be examined by the Supreme Court because a Negro was not a citizen, and therefore could not sue in a federal court.

However, Geyer and Johnson added a new dimension to the case. They attacked the constitutionality of the Missouri Compromise, which prohibited slavery in the territories. Fehrenbacher writes:

Thus, in February 1856, the Dred Scott case and the major political issue of the day had finally converged. From this point on, Sanford became merely the nominal [in name only] defendant. Stricken with mental illness, he would be in an asylum before the end of the year.

Reverdy Johnson had taken up the case at the suggestion of a "southern gentleman" and appropriately so; for the real client that he and Geyer now represented was the slaveholding South.

What had begun as a simple freedom suit now seemed destined to become a case that would determine the validity of the Missouri Compromise. It was still not certain, however, that the Supreme Court would involve itself in this sensitive issue.

The Court Consults

With the attorneys' opening arguments completed, the Court held its first consultation on February 22. Discussion was brief, and the justices reached no conclusions. They met again a few days later to decide on the Court's jurisdiction. In all courts, jurisdiction must be established before a judgment can be made. Jurisdiction means the power of a court to hear and decide cases. During the Court's consultations on *Scott v. Sandford*, then, the first issue to be decided was whether the Court had jurisdiction to hear the case. Should the case be in federal court? This raised the question of whether the Court should review the circuit court's ruling on Negro citizenship. The justices were sharply divided on this question. And with no agreement reached, the Court recessed for the entire month of March.

The Court reconvened in April, but after three consultations the justices were still split on the issue of jurisdiction. In particular, the justices disagreed on whether they should review the lower court's decision on Negro citizenship. A ruling on that decision would determine whether the lower court should have tried the case at all. The question debated by the justices was this: Did the Supreme Court have jurisdiction to decide whether the lower court had had jurisdiction to try Dred Scott's case in the first place?

Four of the nine justices—John McLean and Robert Grier (northerners), John Catron and John Campbell (southerners)— did not think the Court should review the ruling on Negro citizenship. That ruling, they argued, was not being appealed. The only appeal properly before the Court was against the lower court's ruling that Scott was still a slave. Only one issue should concern the Court: Was Dred Scott free or still a slave?

Four other justices—Roger B. Taney, James Wayne, and Peter Daniel (all southerners) and Benjamin Curtis (northerner) argued that the question of the Supreme Court's jurisdiction could not be separated from the citizenship issue. Both must be considered because the ruling on Negro citizenship was a part of the total record sent to the Supreme Court for review.

Samuel Nelson (northerner), who could have broken the tie, was undecided. When the vote remained deadlocked after numerous consultations, Nelson moved that the case be reargued at the Court's next term. And on May 12, after announcing the new delay, Chief Justice Roger Taney instructed the justices and attorneys to consider two questions during the interim.

Negro Citizenship

First, should the Court review the lower court's ruling on Sanford's charge that a Negro could not sue in a federal court because a Negro was not a citizen? After all, the ruling had been in favor of Scott. It was Scott who was appealing the case, and he would not appeal a point that had already been decided in his favor. And Sanford had not appealed it. So, should it now be questioned?

Second, if the Court *was* to consider the issue of Negro citizenship, then it must decide whether the lower court's ruling that a free Negro was a citizen had been correct. Was Dred Scott a citizen of Missouri? If he was not, the Supreme Court did not have jurisdiction to hear the case, because federal jurisdiction depended upon Scott and Sanford's being citizens of different states.

Newspaper reports on the adjournment of Scott's case were mixed as to whether the delay was politically motivated, and historians remain divided on that question. Nevertheless, the fact is

MEMBERS OF THE TANEY COURT

Chief Justice Roger B. Taney (pronounced "tawney") was eighty years old when Dred Scott's case came before the Supreme Court. Taney, appointed by President Andrew Jackson, joined the Court in March 1836, the same month and year that Dred Scott married Harriet Robinson. Taney had previously served as Jackson's attorney general. He had a sharp legal mind, and even his political enemies considered him one of the ablest lawyers in the country. However, Taney believed that the Constitution protected slavery. And his rulings prior to Dred Scott had shown a definite bias on matters relating to slavery and the conflict between North and South.

Associate Justice James Wayne of Georgia was a member of the Supreme Court under Taney.

Three of the associate justices, James M. Wayne of Georgia, John Catron of Tennessee, and John A. Campbell of Alabama, openly defended slavery and its extension into the territories. A fourth justice, Peter V. Daniel of Virginia, was a proslavery fanatic who refused even to set foot on northern soil.

Two of the four remaining justices, Samuel Nelson of New York and Robert C. Grier of Pennsylvania, were northern Democrats who supported states' rights. Although they were not exactly proslavery advocates, they were "grimly anti-antislavery." Benjamin R. Curtis, a Republican from Massachusetts, had displeased his party by supporting the Fugitive Slave Law. However, he shared the party's belief that slavery should not be extended into the territories. Justice John McLean of Ohio was an antislavery Republican with presidential ambitions. He had failed to secure his party's nomination in 1856, but he intended to seek it in 1860.

This, then, was the Court that would decide Dred Scott's fate.

that by the time the Court reconvened, the presidential election of 1856 was over.

Did anyone bother to tell Dred Scott about the adjournment? Did his lawyer try to explain why the case was dragging on for so long? No one knows. If Scott made any comments about his situation, they were never recorded. Meanwhile, he and his family continued to wait.

Chapter 5

Nine Judges and
One Slave

SEVEN MONTHS PASSED BEFORE the Supreme Court reconvened. Events during that interval had not helped Dred
Scott's cause. Inflammatory incidents, which often culminated in
violence, occurred one after the other. Much of the trouble
stemmed from the Kansas-Nebraska Act, passed two years earlier. The act had divided the Nebraska territory into two territories; Kansas and Nebraska. The act in effect repealed the
Missouri Compromise in those areas. Instead of forbidding slavery, it allowed people in the Kansas and Nebraska territories the
right to decide for themselves whether or not they wanted slavery. Debate in Congress had been bitter, and the act passed by a
narrow margin.

Tension sparked by the Kansas-Nebraska Act came to a head
during the seven months Dred Scott waited. In May 1856, a
proslavery mob descended on Lawrence, Kansas. They trashed
the offices and printing presses of the *Free-Soil* newspaper and
destroyed homes and shops. Three nights later, John Brown, a fanatical abolitionist, sought vengeance in a Kansas proslavery set-
tlement. He and his sons dragged five men out of their cabins
and murdered them.

That same week Senator Charles Sumner of Massachusetts
delivered a speech before the Senate arguing for a free Kansas. In
an uncharacteristic outburst of sarcasm he insulted the South and
its leaders, especially Senator Butler of South Carolina. "He has

After challenging another senator on the issue of slavery, Massachusetts senator Charles Sumner was beaten unconscious by Preston Brooks.

chosen a mistress . . . who though ugly to others, is always lovely to him . . . the harlot slavery." Two days later, Representative Preston Brooks of South Carolina, a nephew of Butler out to avenge his uncle's honor, attacked Sumner as he sat at his Senate desk. Using a cane, Brooks beat Sumner into unconsciousness, inflicting injuries from which Sumner never fully recovered.

And just a month before the new court term began, James Buchanan—following a presidential campaign dominated by the slavery issue—was elected president of the United States. Buchanan had been the proslavery Democratic Party's candidate. In this politically supercharged atmosphere, Dred Scott's case would be argued before the Supreme Court for a second time.

Growing Public Awareness of the Dred Scott Trial

Slowly, the press and the public awakened to the growing importance of the Supreme Court's upcoming decision. The *New York Courier* wrote:

Never has the Supreme Court had a case before it so
deeply affecting its own standing before the Nation. . . .
The issue is of vast importance in itself, but there is another problem connected with it of far greater conse-
quence. It is whether the Supreme Court is a political
Court made up of political judges. . . . The Court, in trying this case, is itself on trial.

The issue referred to by the *Courier* was not Dred Scott's
freedom, but whether the Missouri Compromise would be declared unconstitutional. Such a ruling would allow expansion of
slavery into territories where slavery was forbidden.

A Second Attorney for Scott

Soon after the Court reconvened, George Ticknor Curtis, a
Boston attorney and brother of Justice Benjamin Curtis, agreed
to assist with Dred Scott's case. George Curtis enjoyed great respect and prestige as a constitutional and legal authority. His services would be limited to defending Congress's right to pass a
law like the Missouri Compromise that regulated slavery in the
territories—the law on which Dred Scott based his claim to freedom. George Curtis was no abolitionist. He, like his brother, had
supported the Fugitive Slave Act even though a majority of the
people in Massachusetts opposed it. Oddly enough, no
renowned, outright abolitionist ever came forward on Scott's behalf.

Historian Don Fehrenbacher comments on this curious lack
of support:

Now that the political implications of the case were
widely recognized, it became more noticeable that Dred
Scott had no prominent champions of freedom in his cor-
ner. . . . The failure of antislavery radicals to take an earlier interest in the case remains . . . a puzzle. Yet Scott
himself was better off with relatively conservative counsel, for his hope of freedom depended upon the Court's
rising above political and sectional considerations.

Reargument Begins

On Monday, December 15, 1856, reargument of *Dred Scot v. John F. A. Sandford* began. The Court would hear oral arguments for three hours a day. As required by the Court's previous order, the attorneys must first address the rulings made in the lower court regarding Scott's citizenship and his right to bring suit in a federal court.

Montgomery Blair opened for the plaintiff, Dred Scott. He spoke for the full three hours. Blair held that the lower court had already settled the citizenship question. Citizenship could be an issue before the Supreme Court, he argued, only if Sanford had appealed the lower court's ruling. Since Sanford had not appealed, the question of Scott's citizenship could not properly be reviewed by the Court.

Blair said that even though Negroes were segregated socially and denied political rights, they were at the very least "*quasi* citizens." And this limited citizenship gave them certain civil rights, including the right to bring suit in a federal court.

Blair maintained also that the Missouri Compromise was not an issue in Scott's case. Dred Scott, Blair said, had become free when he was taken into Illinois. That freedom had not depended

Montgomery Blair, attorney for Dred Scott, argued that slaves were partial citizens.

upon the constitutionality of any federal law, such as the Missouri Compromise. It was the law of the state of Illinois that forbade slavery, and no one could deny that Illinois had a right to pass such a law.

Second Day

The next day, Tuesday, December 16, Henry Geyer argued for John Sanford. Geyer insisted that the Court must review the lower court's ruling on Negro citizenship. How else, he asked, could the Court determine whether or not it had jurisdiction to hear the case?

Up to this point, the citizenship question had centered on state citizenship. Now Geyer complicated the issue by maintaining that any person involved in a federal suit must be able to prove national as well as state citizenship. A person became a citizen of the United States in two ways, Geyer reminded the Court. One was to be born to that status, and the other was to become a citizen by naturalization. Dred Scott had been born a slave: A slave was not a citizen. And Scott had never been naturalized because only Congress had the power of naturalization.

Therefore, even if Scott's travels onto free soil had made him a free man, they had not made him a citizen of the United States. "A slave, who is not a citizen," Geyer continued, "can not become such by virtue of a deed of manumission or other discharge from bondage."

Geyer then turned to the issue of Dred Scott's freedom. He argued that Scott had not become free because of his residence in Illinois. He acknowledged that Illinois law prevented slavery from being established in that state. But that law did not change the status of someone brought into Illinois who was already a slave, Geyer said. He dismissed Scott's claim to freedom under the Missouri Compromise via his residence at Fort Snelling. The Missouri Compromise was unconstitutional, Geyer declared, because the Constitution did not give Congress power to prohibit slavery anywhere in the country.

Sanford's lawyers could have used the same argument against Dred Scott's becoming free at Fort Snelling as they used regarding his stay in Illinois. But that argument would not have forced a ruling on the Missouri Compromise.

Concerning the sudden focusing on the constitutionality of the Missouri Compromise, Don Fehrenbacher writes:

> The constitutionality of the Missouri Compromise . . . had never been an issue in the earlier deliberations of three courts that [had] heard the case. Neither had it received any special mention in the Supreme Court's order for reargument. Yet this constitutional question, the only subject taken up by all four [lawyers], was now plainly the center of attention. With Dred Scott's private cause converted into a public issue, the courtroom of highest justice had become a political arena.

Sanford's lawyer Reverdy Johnson argued that because they were their owner's property, slaves' status should not change when they were carried over states' borders.

Third Day

On the third day, Sanford's other lawyer, Reverdy Johnson, took up the argument. He spoke mainly on the Missouri Compromise, repeating Geyer's argument that it was unconstitutional because Congress did not have the power to regulate slavery in the territories. However, Article 4 of the Constitution did give Congress the power to make rules and regulations for territories. Johnson, anticipating that Scott's lawyers would counter with that argument, raised the point himself.

Johnson acknowledged that the Constitution gave Congress power to establish temporary governments in territories. But, he argued, that power did not extend to legislation against slavery. Furthermore, such laws were unfair because they deprived southern states of the right to carry their property (slaves) into the territories. The northern states, on the other hand, had no such restriction on their property. Johnson made no distinction between people as property and any other kind of property.

Fourth Day

On the final day, Thursday, December 18, the attorneys concluded their arguments. All four attorneys spoke, although Johnson and Geyer made only brief remarks.

Montgomery Blair held the floor for two hours. He argued that Article 4 not only empowered Congress to establish territorial governments, but also gave Congress authority to "make all needful rules." Congress, he said, was subject only to limitations specifically stated in the Constitution. And nowhere in the Constitution was Congress expressly forbidden to exercise such legislative powers.

With one hour remaining, George Curtis closed out the arguments. He confined his statements to the constitutionality of the Missouri Compromise according to Article 4, section 3 of the Constitution. The second paragraph of section 3 reads in part: "The Congress shall have Power to dispose of and make all needful Rules and Regulations respecting the Territory . . . belonging to the United States."

Curtis reviewed the history of the Missouri Compromise and the circumstances that led to its passage. He referred to debates held at the Constitutional Convention. The framers of the Constitution, Curtis said, intended that Congress should have full authority over a territory as long as it remained a territory. Only when a territory becomes a state can it establish its own laws. Therefore, the Missouri Compromise was constitutional, and Dred Scott was entitled to his freedom because of his residence at Fort Snelling in free Wisconsin territory.

Into the Hands of the Court

With the conclusion of George Curtis's argument, both sides' case was complete. In keeping with the ever-increasing interest in the Dred Scott trial, newspapers across the country printed the arguments and speculated on the possible verdict. The general consensus was that Dred Scott would not be granted his freedom. "It seems to be the impression," wrote Montgomery Blair, "that the Court will be adverse to my client and to the power of Congress over the Territories [that is, the Missouri Compromise]."

The Dred Scott trial was delayed because Justice Peter Daniel's (pictured) wife died in a fire in the family's home in Washington.

But almost two months passed before the justices met to discuss how they would rule on the Dred Scott case. Tragedy caused the delay: In early January 1857, Justice Peter Daniel's wife died in a fire in the family home in Washington. Daniel suffered burns when he tried to rescue her. The Court delayed discussion until he had recovered sufficiently from his injuries and personal grief to resume his duties. Finally on February 14, 1857, all nine justices were available, and the Court began its deliberations.

Options of the Court

The Dred Scott case now addressed far more than Dred Scott the person. It had evolved into a consideration of three major issues: 1) Negro citizenship; 2) the status of slaves held on free soil; and 3) the constitutionality of laws that prohibited slavery in the territories. The Court could decide the case by ruling on the first question only, the second question only, or all three.

The justices could choose to reverse the lower federal court's ruling on Negro citizenship and dismiss the case, leaving Scott a slave. Or they could rule that whereas Scott had a right to free-dom when he lived in free territory, he lost that freedom when he returned to Missouri. Thus, the Court could decide Scott's fate without ruling on the constitutionality of the Missouri Compro-mise. However, because the main function of the Supreme Court is to settle constitutional questions, many expected a ruling on that law.

The justices could also overturn the lower court's verdict that Scott was still a slave. They could rule that Scott's residence in Illinois and at Fort Snelling had made him free regardless of where he lived later. However, such a ruling was highly unlikely considering the majority of southern justices on the Court.

A Court Divided

The Court considered first the question of jurisdiction regarding the lower court's ruling on Negro citizenship. On this point the justices deadlocked just as they had in April 1856, with a mix of northerners and southerners on each side.

However, regarding the Missouri Compromise, which pre-vented the expansion of slavery, the five southern justices in a bloc wanted to declare it unconstitutional. Northern justices Curtis and McLean would have upheld it. Northerners Nelson and Grier urged the Court not to rule on the Compromise at all, but to simply uphold the lower court's decision that under Mis-souri law Dred Scott was still a slave. By a vote of five to four, Nelson and Grier prevailed. It appeared that the Court would avoid ruling on the controversial issues of Negro citizenship and the constitutionality of the Missouri Compromise.

Having supposedly reached a decision, Justice Nelson was assigned to write the Court's majority opinion. Nelson began work immediately, but within five days the Court would change its mind. What happened during those five days?

Pressure on the Court

Historical evidence indicates that the Court—especially the south-ern justices—was pressured to force a decision on the Missouri Compromise. For example, Alexander Stephens, a congressman from Georgia, wrote to his brother: "I have been urging all the influences I could bring to bear upon the Supreme Court to get them to postpone no longer the case on the Missouri Restriction before them, but to decide it." Stephens probably pressured his fellow Georgian, Justice Wayne, who proved to be an important figure in the Court's impending change of heart.

Pressure came also from President-elect James Buchanan. He had won election on the promise "to destroy the dangerous slavery agitation and thus restore peace." If the Supreme Court ruled on the Missouri Compromise before his inauguration on March 4, he could defer to its decision rather than make any politically risky, controversial statements of his own.

In a highly improper move, Buchanan wrote a letter to his longtime friend on the Supreme Court, southerner John Catron, inquiring about the status of the case. Catron answered with what must have been disappointing news for Buchanan: The Court would not rule on the Missouri Compromise. However, only five days after Nelson had been instructed to write the Court's opinion, Catron wrote to Buchanan again. This time, Catron said the Court *would* rule on the Missouri Compromise.

Chapter 6

The Opinion of
the Court

JUSTICE NELSON HAD ALREADY BEGUN to write the Court's
opinion when Justice James Wayne of Georgia moved for
Chief Justice Taney to write the Court's opinion instead of Nelson. And Wayne specified that the chief justice should cover *all*
the main issues raised in the case. In other words, the opinion
should include judgments on Negro citizenship and on the Missouri Compromise. Wayne wrote later that the motion was his
own idea, but historians speculate that Taney may have been
working behind the scenes.

Put to a vote, Wayne's motion passed. McLean and Curtis rejected the motion, Grier was undecided, and Nelson, being ill,
was not present. Walter Ehrlich writes in *They Have No Rights*:

> The remaining five [justices], then—Taney, Wayne,
> Catron, Campbell, and Daniel—*the five justices who came
> from slave states*—formed the bare majority that now de-
> cided it could peacefully settle the slavery issue by declar-
> ing the Missouri Compromise unconstitutional. This was
> the turn of events that enabled Wayne to say he had gained
> not only a great triumph for the South, but also a very im-
> portant point for the peace and quiet of the country.

The Weak Link

Although the motion passed and Chief Justice Taney would now
write the opinion, a problem remained for the southern justices.

Upon being asked to alter his opinion by President James Buchanan, Justice Robert Grier (pictured) ruled against Dred Scott.

Five of nine was not an impressive majority for such an important decision. Consequently, pressure was brought to bear on Justice Robert Grier, among the four northerners the justice considered the most likely to be swayed. Privately, he believed that the Missouri Compromise was unconstitutional. But he had preferred to avoid controversy and bypass the issue completely. Justice Catron wrote again to Buchanan, asking the president-elect to "drop Grier a line, saying how necessary it is—and how good the opportunity is, to settle the agitation by an affirmative decision of the Supreme Court."

Buchanan wrote to Grier immediately, and on February 23 Grier wrote Buchanan that he had shown the letter "to our mutual friends [Justice] Wayne and the Chief Justice." The two men must have been persuasive, because Grier ended his letter with this confidential disclosure:

> On conversation with the chief justice, I have agreed to concur with him. . . . There will therefore be six, if not seven (perhaps Nelson will remain neutral) who will decide the Compromise law of 1820 to be of *non-effect*. . . . We will not let any others of our brethren know anything about *the cause of our anxiety* to produce this result, and though contrary to our usual practice, we . . . thought it due to you to state to you in candor and confidence the real state of the matter.

The Supreme Court's decision would not be announced until after Buchanan was sworn in as president. However, Buchanan

Upon being assured that the Supreme Court would not vote in favor of Dred Scott, James Buchanan could confidently say that he would submit to whatever decision the Court arrived at in the case.

now knew what to say in his inaugural address. Regarding the case pending before the Supreme Court, he told the inaugural crowd that a verdict would soon be rendered by the Supreme Court on the question of slavery in the territories. "To their decision, in common with all good citizens, I shall cheerfully submit, whatever this [decision] may be." It was a misleading, hypocritical statement, because the president knew exactly what the Court's decision would be. Two days later, the verdict was announced.

The Final Verdict

On March 6, 1857, eleven years after Dred Scott first sued for freedom, Chief Justice Taney read the long-awaited verdict. The courtroom was filled to capacity. The eighty-year-old chief justice read for two hours, his voice faint from fatigue.

In summary, the Court's rulings according to Chief Justice Taney were as follows:

1. RULING: The Supreme Court had jurisdiction to review the lower court's ruling on Negro citizenship.

REASONING: If the lower court had erred in its ruling that Dred Scott was a citizen, then neither it nor the Supreme Court had jurisdiction to hear the case. Jurisdiction could be determined only by reviewing the lower court's ruling.

2. RULING: Negroes were not citizens of the United States and therefore had no right to bring suit in a federal court. Consequently, the lower federal court had erred in its ruling on Negro citizenship and had never had jurisdiction to hear the case.

ROGER B. TANEY, CHIEF JUSTICE

Roger Taney has sometimes been described as antislavery because he freed his own slaves. However, his judicial decisions do not support that characterization. Nor does this unpublished opinion he wrote in 1832 when he was President Andrew Jackson's attorney general:

> The African race in the United States even when free, are everywhere a degraded class, and exercise no political influence. The privileges they are allowed to enjoy are accorded to them as a matter of kindness . . . rather than of right. They are the only class of persons who can be held as mere property, as slaves. . . . They were not looked upon as citizens by [those] who formed the Constitution. They were evidently not supposed to be included by the term *citizens*.

Historians consider the Dred Scott ruling a blemish on the otherwise admirable career of Roger Taney.

Twenty-five years later Taney's ruling on Negro citizenship in the Dred Scott decision showed he still believed that slavery was protected by the Constitution.

Taney's reputation as a great jurist suffered in the years following the Dred Scott decision. However, twentieth-century historians have reevaluated his place in history. It is generally conceded that he had a fine legal mind and that his achievements during his twenty-nine-year tenure as chief justice were substantial. One of the most important achievements of the Taney Court was in balancing the power of the federal government to regulate interstate commerce with the state governments' power to protect the health and welfare of their citizens.

Taney's accomplishments were many, and he might have been remembered as a great Supreme Court justice. "If you could take [Dred Scott] off his record," Professor Walter Ehrlich has said, "he would undoubtedly stand with John Marshall as one of the great chief justices of the Supreme Court. But you can't take away Dred Scott."

REASONING: "[Negroes] are not included, and were not meant to be included under the word 'citizens' in the Constitution, and can therefore claim none of [its] rights and privileges."

In his book *America in 1857: A Nation on the Brink*, Professor Kenneth Stampp makes the following comment regarding this ruling on Negro citizenship:

> The path to [Taney's] startling opinion was littered with misrepresentations of the status of both slaves and free blacks in the late eighteenth century, with other historical inaccuracies, and with confusing statements about the nature and origin of state and federal citizenship. To bolster his opinion Taney rewrote the Declaration of Independence to read "all *white* men are created equal," and he amended the Constitution to transform it into a racist document.

3. RULING: Dred Scott had not become a free man during his residence at Fort Snelling despite his claim of freedom under the Missouri Compromise.

REASONING: The Missouri Compromise had been unconstitutional from the beginning because it violated the Fifth Amendment, which asserts that "No person shall be . . . deprived of . . . property without due process of law." (Taney made no distinction between humans as property and other forms of property.) It was the first time since 1803 that the Court had ruled an act of Congress null and void.

4. RULING: Dred Scott was not free as a result of his residence in Illinois.

REASONING: When Scott returned to Missouri, he became a slave again because his status there depended upon the law of Missouri, where slavery was legal.

In sum, Dred Scott was "not a citizen . . . and the Circuit Court of the United States, for that reason, had no jurisdiction in the case, and could give no judgment in it." The suit must be returned to the lower court with instructions that it be dismissed.

Dissent

The two dissenting justices, John McLean and Benjamin Curtis, each presented lengthy statements explaining why they disagreed with the Court's ruling. Of the two, Curtis's was considered the most effective.

Curtis responded to Taney's assertion that the Constitution denied citizenship to freed slaves. The Constitution, Curtis said, did not deny citizenship to anyone who already possessed it. And under the Articles of Confederation, which had preceded the Constitution, such citizenship had existed. In five states, Negroes had not only been recognized as citizens but "possessed the franchise [right to vote] . . . on equal terms with other citizens."

Therefore, according to Curtis, the lower federal court's ruling that free Negroes were citizens had been correct. "My opinion," he said, "is that, under the Constitution of the United States, every free person born on the soil of a State, who is a citizen of that State by force of its . . . laws, is also a citizen of the United States."

Curtis argued also that the Court had no right to rule on the Missouri Compromise. The chief justice, Curtis implied, could have not have it both ways. He could not rule that the Supreme Court did not have jurisdiction to hear the case, and then proceed to rule on both the consequences of Scott's residence on free soil and on the Missouri Compromise, as though the Court *did* have jurisdiction. "In my opinion," Curtis stated, "the judgment of the Circuit Court [which declared Scott still a slave] should be reversed, and the [case sent back] for a new trial."

However, the majority had spoken. After eleven years, Dred Scott finally had his answer. He was still a slave. And furthermore, the law of the land now appeared to legalize slavery everywhere.

What Did the Court Decide?

But was the Supreme Court's ruling the law of the land? Had the majority of the Court spoken? Was the majority opinion read by Taney on March 6 truly the Court's opinion? Or was it the opinion of the chief justice? Was Taney speaking obiter dictum (that is, incidentally passing judgment on issues not on trial) as the antislavery Republicans charged? Or, as others argued, was the constitutionality of the Missouri Compromise and the question of black citizenship legitimately before the Court? These questions were asked in 1857, and they continue to be debated by historians today.

"Opinion of the Court" implies that the majority of the justices agreed. However, that was not the case. All eight of the associate justices wrote opinions, and only two of them agreed with everything Taney said. And only three agreed with Taney's state-

Only three out of eight of the Supreme Court justices agreed with Roger Taney that Negroes of African descent could not be citizens, whether free or slave.

ment that Negroes of African descent could not be citizens, *whether free or slave.* What part of the Dred Scott decision, then, was binding?

Of the Court's four rulings, only the ruling that Dred Scott remained a slave has been unanimously accepted by legal scholars as a majority ruling of the Court. Beyond that, historians have never agreed on whether the other three rulings represented the majority opinion. However, what is important is that most people in 1857—both in the North and the South—accepted Taney's opinion as the opinion of the Court.

But whether the Dred Scott verdict was reached by one man or by a Court majority, it did not answer the crucial question: Is it morally right for one human being to hold another in slavery? That question still faced the nation, because the Dred Scott decision neither settled the issue of slavery nor prevented a civil war, as some had hoped.

Reaction to the Court's Decision

The Supreme Court's verdict was met with anger in the North and with jubilation in the South.

Republican newspapers expressed outrage at the racist implication of the Court's decision. The *New York Tribune* wrote:

> A negro, because of his color, is denied the rights of a citizen of the United States—even the right to sue in our Courts for the redress [correction] of the most flagrant wrongs. . . . The decision . . . is entitled to just as much moral weight as would be the judgment of a majority of those congregated in any Washington bar-room.

And the *Chicago Tribune* leveled even harsher judgment:

> This decision has sapped the Constitution of its glorious and distinctive features, and seeks to pervert it into a barbarous and unchristian channel. . . . To say . . . that a Free People can respect or will obey a decision so fraught with disastrous consequences to the People and their Liberties, is to dream of impossibilities.

Most of the southern newspapers approved the Supreme Court's action. The *Charleston Daily Courier* in South Carolina declared that the decision "will . . . settle these vexed questions [constitutionality of the Missouri Compromise and Negro citizenship] forever, quiet the country . . . and tend greatly to perpetuate our Union."

The *Constitutionalist* of Augusta, Georgia, wrote: "Southern opinion upon the subject of southern slavery . . . is now the supreme law of the land . . . and opposition to southern opinion upon this subject is now opposition to the Constitution, and morally treason against the Government."

Antislavery pastors denounced the Court's decision in their Sunday sermons, and soon articles, pamphlets, and books began appearing in great numbers. Although some of the writings defended the decision, the greater number were written by those critical of the ruling.

"This Atrocious Decision"

The response by free Negroes to a Supreme Court decision that denied citizenship to themselves and their children was hard, cold anger. The following resolutions presented at a Negro protest meeting held at Israel Church in Philadelphia are typical of Negro reaction to the Dred Scott decision:

> *Resolved,* that this atrocious decision furnishes final confirmation of the already well-known fact that, under the Constitution and government of the United States, the colored people are nothing and can be nothing but an alien, disfranchised, and degraded class.

> *Resolved,* that to attempt . . . to prove that there is no support given to slavery in the Constitution . . . is to argue against common sense, [and] to ignore history . . . and that while it may suit white men, who do not feel the iron heel, to please themselves with such theories, it ill becomes the man of color, whose daily experience refutes the absurdity, to indulge in such idle fantasies.

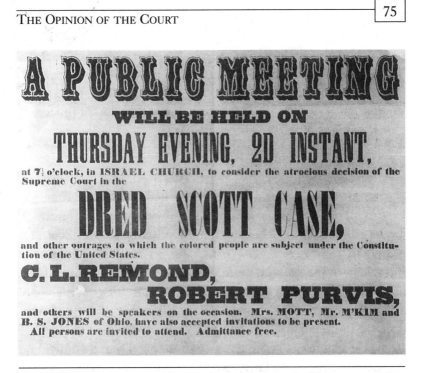

The Dred Scott decision created an attitude of increased militancy among free Negroes.

Resolved that no allegiance is due from any man, or any class of men, to a government founded and administered in iniquity, and that the only duty the colored man owes to a Constitution under which he is declared to be an inferior and degraded being . . . is to denounce and repudiate it, and to do what he can by all proper means to bring it into contempt.

Don Fehrenbacher describes the effect of the Dred Scott decision on free Negroes:

For the free Negro community especially, this "judicial incarnation of wolfishness," as Frederick Douglass called it, seems to have inspired a sudden shift to a higher level of militancy. Words of defiance rang out at numerous protest meetings, and it was as a response to the Dred Scott decision that black abolitionists organized a celebration of "Crispus Attucks Day" on March 5, 1858, in

Boston's cradle of liberty, Faneuil Hall. This spectacular meeting honoring the Negro killed in the Boston Massacre was "a feast of sight and sound," repeated every year until ratification of the Fifteenth Amendment [guaranteeing the right to vote] in 1870.

Free at Last

Shortly after the Court announced its decision, Irene Emerson Chaffee transferred ownership of Dred Scott and his family to Taylor Blow. And on May 26, 1857, Dred and Harriet Scott appeared in the Circuit Court of St. Louis County with Taylor Blow, who formally freed them. In accordance with Missouri law, the Scotts had to post a thousand-dollar bond for good behavior in order to remain in St. Louis. Taylor Blow agreed to be responsible for the bond amount, should it ever become necessary.

According to the scant accounts available, Dred Scott worked as a hotel porter, and Harriet as a washerwoman. About a month after Scott received his freedom, a reporter from *Leslie's Illustrated Newspaper* approached the Scotts seeking their photograph. Harriet was reluctant because promoters were pressuring Dred to go on a publicity tour through the North, which she opposed. Ultimately, she agreed to let the family be photographed, and pictures of Dred, Harriet, and their two daughters appeared in the June 27, 1857, issue of *Leslie's Illustrated Newspaper*. A St. Louis artist later painted a portrait of Dred Scott from the photograph.

Sadly, Dred Scott lived less than a year and a half after receiving his freedom. He died of tuberculosis on September 17, 1858. As for those who had played a part in his drama, all were affected in one way or another by their involvement in one of the most important trials in America's history.

Young Benjamin Curtis, one of the dissenting justices, was virtually forced by Taney to resign from the Supreme Court. Uncomfortable with the continued hostility of the chief justice, Curtis resigned from the Court five months after the Dred Scott verdict.

John F. A. Sanford died in an insane asylum two months after the Supreme Court decision.

The paper that formally freed Dred Scott and his wife Harriet from slavery. After fighting for his freedom for so many years, Scott lived less than a year and a half after being freed.

Calvin Chaffee, the physician and antislavery congressman married to the former Irene Emerson, never ran for office again. Despite denials of having had any knowledge of his wife's ownership of Dred Scott, his political career was over. He later resumed his medical practice.

Irene Emerson Chaffee—whom Scott had first sued for his freedom—lived until 1903, surviving Scott by forty-five years.

Both Charles Drake, the attorney who helped Dred Scott initiate his suit for freedom, and Reverdy Johnson, Sanford's attorney in the Supreme Court, served on the powerful Joint Committee on Reconstruction after the Civil War.

Taylor Blow was a southern sympathizer during the Civil War. In 1867 he filed bankruptcy, and he died one year later. Taylor's older brother Henry became a Republican and worked to prevent Missouri's secession from the Union. He served two terms in Congress and was also a member of the Joint Committee on Reconstruction.

And what of the Supreme Court that had condemned Dred Scott to slavery? By the time the Civil War began, Peter Daniel, the fanatical proslavery justice, and John McLean, who had wanted to be president, had both died. Justice John Campbell resigned at the outbreak of the Civil War so that he could serve the Confederacy. James Wayne, John Catron, and Robert Grier remained on the Court, becoming strong supporters of the Union. Roger Taney remained as chief justice—"unrepentant and unredeemed"—until he died in 1864, the fourth year of the Civil War.

Epitaph for a Slave

Dred Scott's wife, Harriet, and his daughter Eliza survived him by only a few years. The remaining daughter, Lizzie, married Henry Madison of St. Louis, and her descendants attended centennial observances held there in 1957. In a commemorative ceremony on March 6, 1957—one hundred years after Dred Scott was told he was not, and never could be, a citizen of the United States—a granite headstone donated by a granddaughter of Taylor Blow was placed on Dred Scott's unmarked grave.

The inscription on the front reads:

DRED SCOTT
BORN ABOUT 1799
DIED SEPT. 17. 1858
Freed from slavery by
his friend Taylor Blow

and on the back:

DRED SCOTT
SUBJECT OF THE DECISION OF
THE SUPREME COURT OF THE
UNITED STATES IN 1857 WHICH
DENIED CITIZENSHIP TO THE
NEGRO, VOIDED THE MISSOURI
COMPROMISE ACT, BECAME
ONE OF THE EVENTS THAT
RESULTED IN THE CIVIL WAR

Epilogue

Dred Scott's
Long Shadow

THE DRED SCOTT DECISION REMAINS an ugly blot on the history of the Supreme Court. For several generations after the Dred Scott trial, the Court's reputation suffered. Noted Civil War historian Bruce Catton writes:

President Lincoln and his advisers confer prior to the signing of the Emancipation Proclamation, which abolished slavery in the United States.

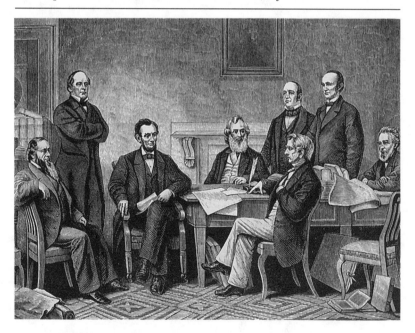

Members of the House of Representatives react after the passage of the Emancipation Proclamation.

The Court's prestige suffered immensely, and Justice Felix Frankfurter [associate justice from 1939 to 1962], once remarked that after the Civil War justices of the Supreme Court never mentioned the Dred Scott case, any more than a family in which a son had been hanged mentioned ropes and scaffolds.

And in the end, the Court's ruling settled little. Slavery continued to divide the country. The problem was resolved not by

Roger Taney and his Court but by a Civil War that cost six hundred thousand Americans their lives and resulted in the Thirteenth Amendment to the Constitution. The amendment proclaimed that "neither slavery nor involuntary servitude . . . shall exist within the United States." It was ratified on December 6, 1865.

The Dred Scott decision itself was overturned in 1866. That year Congress passed the Civil Rights Act, which guaranteed citizenship to blacks and prohibited discrimination on the grounds of race or color. Two years later, the Fourteenth Amendment gave the act constitutional protection by affirming that "all persons born or naturalized in the United States . . . are citizens of the United States and of the State wherein they reside." (Roger Taney, who had ruled that African Americans could not be citizens, had died two years before.)

The appalling decision, which had denied justice to a large segment of America's people, was corrected. But it would not be forgotten. "The tragedy of Dred Scott," writes historian Philip B. Kurland, "remains a ghost of terrifying proportions."

More than a century has passed since Lincoln's Emancipation Proclamation and the Thirteenth Amendment prohibited slavery in the United States. However, as historians Samuel Eliot Morison and Henry Steele Commager write: "We now know that the slavery question was but one aspect of a race and class problem that is still far from [a] solution." Dred Scott, and all that his struggle represented, continues to cast a long shadow.

Chronology

ca. 1800

Dred Scott born.

1820

Congress enacts Missouri Compromise.

1830

Mexico abolishes slavery in Texas.

1831

William Garrison begins publishing the *Liberator;* Dred Scott's owners, Peter and Elizabeth Blow, die; Dred Scott is sold to John Emerson.

1833

American Anti-Slavery Society founded; Dred Scott taken into free state of Illinois.

1836

Texas declares independence from Mexico; Dred Scott taken into free Wisconsin territory; marries Harriet Robinson.

1838

Irene Sanford marries John Emerson.

1840

Irene Emerson, with Dred and Harriet Scott, returns to the slave state of Missouri.

1843

John Emerson dies.

1846

United States goes to war with Mexico; Dred and Harriet Scott file freedom suit against Irene Emerson in Missouri state circuit court.

1848

First Missouri Supreme Court appeal.

1850

Second state circuit court trial; second Missouri Supreme Court appeal; Irene Emerson marries Calvin Chaffee, moves to Massachusetts, and turns her business affairs over to her brother, John Sanford; Compromise of 1850 is enacted.

1852

Harriet Beecher Stowe publishes antislavery novel *Uncle Tom's Cabin*.

1854

U. S. federal circuit court trial of *Dred Scott v. John F. A. Sandford*; Kansas-Nebraska Act passed.

1856

John Brown's massacre; Sumner-Brooks incident in Washington, D. C.; James Buchanan elected president; *Dred Scott v. John F. A. Sandford* argued before U.S. Supreme Court.

1857

Dred Scott decision; Taylor Blow formally frees Dred and Harriet Scott.

1858

Dred Scott dies.

1861

Civil War begins.

1863

Emancipation Proclamation is issued.

1865

Thirteenth Amendment abolishes slavery in the United States.

1866

Civil Rights Act.

1868

Fourteenth Amendment guarantees citizenship to all persons born or naturalized in the United States.

For Further Reading

Patricia Beatty, *Jayhawker*. New York: Morrow Junior Books, 1991. An historical novel set in the early years of the Civil War. Lije Tulley is a teenage Kansas farm boy and a fierce abolitionist determined to put an end to slavery. He becomes a Jayhawker. (Jayhawkers are Kansas abolitionist raiders intent on freeing slaves from the neighboring state of Missouri.) As a Jayhawker, Lije encounters grave danger when he is sent to join and spy on a Confederate group. The group includes ruthless renegade, Charley Quantrill, a mysterious sharpshooter known as Jim Hickok, and a sullen teenager by the name of Jesse James. An exciting, suspenseful, and historically accurate story.

Richard B. Bernstein and Jerome Agel, *Into the Third Century: The Supreme Court*. New York: Walker and Company, 1989. A clearly written history of the Supreme Court. Describes the Court's origins, includes biographies of influential justices throughout the Court's history, and assesses the modern court.

William Dudley, ed., *Slavery: Opposing Viewpoints*. San Diego: Greenhaven Press, 1992. This anthology includes authors of varied and contrasting opinions, including Abraham Lincoln and Roger Taney, presenting the reader with arguments on different sides of the slavery issue.

Suzanne Freedman, *Roger Taney: The Dred Scott Legacy*. Springfield, NJ: Enslow Publishers, 1995. A balanced account of Roger Taney's background and experience in the judicial system, focusing on his role in the Dred Scott case.

D. J. Herda, *The Dred Scott Case: Slavery and Citizenship*. Hillside, NJ: Enslow Publishers, 1994. This book, targeted for young adults, covers Dred Scott's case as well as his early life and the circumstances leading up to the case, and the events following the decision.

Julius Lester, *To Be a Slave*. New York: Scholastic, 1968. Edited firsthand accounts of slavery. Admirably balanced reports of both planter atrocities and kindnesses. Highly readable and insightfully annotated.

Marc McCutcheon, *Everyday Life in the 1800s.* Cincinnati, OH: Writer's Digest Books, 1993. Provides a wealth of extremely interesting, out-of-the-way facts about slang, transportation, homes, fashions, occupations, and much more.

L. H. Ofosu-Appiah, *People in Bondage: African Slavery Since the 15th Century.* Minneapolis, MN: Runestone Press, 1993. A history of the enslavement of Africans in different places and different cultures, how it happened and what it was like. Concludes with a discussion about current chattel slavery and forced-labor camps. A very readable book that shows slavery is not unique to the history of the United States.

James Rogers, *The Antislavery Movement.* New York: Facts On File, 1994. An overview of the antislavery movement in the United States. Includes chapters on slave life during the Civil War, as well as the lives of freed slaves during the Reconstruction period. The final chapter deals with the troubled and often slow progress toward civil rights. Includes documented footnotes at the end of each chapter.

Works Consulted

Mortimer J. Adler, ed., *A House Dividing*. Vol. 8 of *The Annals of America*, 1850–1857. Chicago: Encyclopaedia Britannica, 1968. This eighth of eighteen volumes contains letters, tracts, documents, poems, and first-person accounts of historical events.

Frederick S. Allis Jr., "The Dred Scott Labyrinth," in *Teachers of History: Essays in Honor of Laurence Bradford Packard*, ed. H. Stuart Hughes. New York: Cornell University Press, 1954. A highly readable, sometimes humorous essay that helps the reader understand the confusing and complex issues that pervade the Dred Scott trial.

Irving H. Bartlett, *The American Mind in the Mid–Nineteenth Century*. New York: Thomas Y. Crowell Company, 1967. This title in the Crowell American History Series examines the political, philosophical, and social thought of mid-nineteenth-century America.

Thomas Hart Benton, *Historical and Legal Examination of that part of the Decision of the Supreme Court of the United States in the Dred Scott Case, Which Declares the Unconstitutionality of the Missouri Compromise Act, and the Self-Extension of the Constitution to Territories, Carrying Slavery Along With It*. 1857. Reprint, New York: Kraus Reprint Company, 1969. A contemporary account by a respected former U. S. senator. It is a scathing attack on Chief Justice Taney's decision in the Dred Scott case. Originally published before the Civil War.

Ray A. Billington, *American History Before 1877*. Totowa, NJ: Rowman & Littlefield, 1965. A history in outline form with interpretative sections throughout relating past events to the present. Helpful bibliography at the end of each chapter.

Paul F. Boller Jr. and Ronald Story, eds., *A More Perfect Union: Documents in U.S. History*. Vol. 1, to 1877. Boston: Houghton

Mifflin, 1984. Contains the less familiar as well as the familiar documents that illustrate America's political and social history to 1877.

Bruce Catton, "The Dred Scott Case," in *Quarrels That Have Shaped the Constitution*, ed. John A. Garraty. New York: Harper & Row, 1962. Examines the personal and political conflicts that led to the Supreme Court's verdict in the Dred Scott case.

Benjamin Robbins Curtis Jr., ed., *A Memoir of Benjamin Robbins Curtis, With Some of His Professional and Miscellaneous Writings.* Vol. 2. New York: Da Capo Press, 1970. Memoir, writings, and speeches of one of the two dissenting associate justices in *Dred Scott v. John F. A. Sandford.*

Walter Ehrlich, *They Have No Rights: Dred Scott's Struggle for Freedom.* West Port, CT: Greenwood Press, 1979. A thorough, step-by-step account beginning with Dred Scott's birth and ending with his death. Documents trials from the initial suit in the Missouri State Circuit Court through the U. S. Supreme Court.

Don E. Fehrenbacher, *The Dred Scott Case: Its Significance in American Law and Politics.* New York: Oxford University Press, 1978. Pulitzer Prize–winning, definitive work on the Dred Scott case. Comprehensive, well-balanced study of the legal and political background of the case and its legal and political consequences.

Don E. Fehrenbacher, ed., *Abraham Lincoln: A Documentary Portrait Through His Speeches and Writings.* New York: The New American Library of World Literature, 1964. Selected speeches and letters of Abraham Lincoln. Contains a helpful introduction by the editor.

Paul Finkelman, *Slavery in the Courtroom: An Annotated Bibliography of American Cases.* Washington, DC: Library of Congress, 1985. Collection of annotated, uncataloged pamphlets on cases dealing with all aspects of slavery.

Mary Ann Harrell, *Equal Justice Under Law: The Supreme Court in American Life.* Washington, DC: The Supreme Court Historical Society with the cooperation of the National Geographic Society, 1974. A well-written and richly illustrated history of the Supreme Court and its major cases. Also examines the Court's role in modern society.

Vincent C. Hopkins, *Dred Scott's Case.* New York: Atheneum, 1967. A detailed study of the background of the Dred Scott case and the Supreme Court trial.

Stanley I. Kutler, ed., *The Dred Scott Decision: Law or Politics?* Boston: Houghton Mifflin, 1967. Contains excerpts from opinions of Chief Justice Taney and the dissenting justices, Curtis and Nelson, as well as newspaper accounts of the day and reactions of politicians and the legal community. Includes historical essays reflecting multiple views regarding the Supreme Court's verdict. Comprehensive introduction by the editor.

Katherine J. Lee, *Courts and Judges: How They Work.* A Citizens Legal Manual by HALT, Inc., and Organization of Americans for Legal Reform. Washington, DC: HALT, May 1987. Easy-to-understand description of how the state and federal courts of the American judicial system work.

Walker Lewis, *Without Fear or Favor: A Biography of Chief Justice Roger Brooke Taney.* Boston: Houghton Mifflin, 1965. A complete account of the career of the chief justice.

Samuel Eliot Morison, *The Oxford History of the American People.* Vol. 2. 1965. Reprint, New York: Penguin Books, 1972. In this volume, the Pulitzer Prize–winning historian presents a comprehensive history of the American people from the election of George Washington as first president of the United States though the Civil War and its aftermath. A clear, readable book.

Samuel Eliot Morison and Henry Steele Commager, *The Growth of the American Republic.* 5th ed. Vol. 1. New York: Oxford University Press, 1962. Overview of American history from 1492 through Lincoln's assassination in 1865.

Kenneth M. Stampp, *America in 1857: A Nation on the Brink*. New York: Oxford University Press, 1990. A well-documented, in-depth account of a year of significant events and issues that led to the Civil War.

James Brewer Stewart, *Holy Warriors: The Abolitionists and American Slavery*. New York: Hill and Wang, 1976. History of abolitionism in America and the founding of the American Anti-Slavery Society.

Charles Warren, *The Supreme Court in United States History*. Vol. 2, 1836-1918. Boston: Little, Brown, 1922. Contains a wide assortment of journalistic reactions to the Dred Scott decision.

Index

Picture Credits

Cover photo: The Bettmann Archive

Archive Photos, 9, 26, 45, 47, 54, 61, 63

Archives, Langston Hughes Memorial Library, Lincoln University, PA, 75

The Bettmann Archive, 37

Corbis-Bettmann, 29, 34, 67, 69

Library of Congress, 36

Missouri Historical Society, 24, 77

North Wind Picture Archives, 13, 30, 50, 57, 80, 81

Stock Montage, Inc., 14, 16, 22 (both), 59, 72

About the Author

Bonnie L. Lukes is a freelance writer living in southern California. She graduated from California State University, Northridge, with a major in English literature.

She has published another book for Lucent Books, *The American Revolution*, as well as essays and stories in a wide variety of magazines and newspapers. Her book *How to Be A Reasonably Thin Teenage Girl* was chosen by the National Council of Books for Children as an Outstanding Science Trade Book.